The Gay Agenda 2014

Don't Stop

Juan Ahonen-Jover, Ph.D.

Published by **create**space
Second Edition

Book website: www.GayAgenda2014.com

Dedication

This book is for all persons who
believe in the equality expressed in the
United States Declaration of Independence—

**"We hold these truths to be self-evident, that all men are
created equal"—**

and in the United States Constitution:

**"Nor deny to any person within its jurisdiction the equal
protection of the laws."**

Books in This Series

The Gay Agenda 2012: All Out

The Gay Agenda 2013: All In

The Gay Agenda 2014: Don't Stop

The Gay Agenda is the most comprehensive guidebook for achieving legal equality for lesbian, gay, bisexual, and transgender Americans (LGBT). The only book like it, it gets updated yearly with specific action plans for that year.

What Readers Are Saying

"Unprecedented. Now in its third year, there is nothing like this book."

"I was also thrilled by your book, 'The Gay Agenda,' so open, so frank, such empowering ideas. An iconic guidebook for a movement that's now unstoppable."

"It may be the first book that tells the unvarnished truth!"

"It is a compendium/combination of all of the following: an Op Ed, a manual, encyclopedia article, memoir, pep talk."

"The book will be a wonderful resource to anyone who cares about achieving full equality."

"You have certainly tackled a HUGE and BROAD topic and done a marvelous job."

"It is definitely an easy read since the chapters are only two or three pages long!"

"Such a terrific project, book, contribution!!!!"

Is This Book for *You?*

This book is for believers only. Do you firmly believe in the principle of treating everybody equally under the law?

- If you are seeking to understand the most important social issue of our generation, this book is for you (especially Part I and the epilogue).

- If you are a parent or grandparent interested in family values and protecting your children, this book is for you (especially Parts I, II, and the epilogue).

- If you are a policy maker, independently of party affiliation, who wants to write laws that are fair, this book is for you (read it all).

- If you are a religious person interested in preserving your freedom of religion, this book is for you (especially Part I and the epilogue).

- If your sexual orientation or gender identity or expression does not fit that of the majority, this book is for you. You may know some of the information presented, but you will gain insights and inspiration for fighting for equal treatment under the law (so read it all and *take action*).

- If you are a believer in equality, this book is for you. You may know some of the book's content, but read it all and *take action.*

- If you have read the 2012 or 2013 editions of *The Gay Agenda*, read Part IV in detail since it describes the actions to take in 2014.

Contents

Preface

In the United States, our core beliefs are under attack. Freedom of religion is under attack. Family values are under attack. Individualism and the pursuit of happiness are under attack. The courts are under attack. This book reveals what freedom of religion is really like, what real family values are, what genuine individualism and actual pursuit of happiness are, and what the role of the courts is.

The *Gay Agenda* book series is for people who believe in the core principle of our Constitution: to be treated equally under the law. What would it be like if we could return to the vision of our great Constitution? A vision of freedom, including freedom of religion and freedom to individuality.

The *Gay Agenda 2014: Don't Stop* describes in detail the gay agenda—what it is and what needs to be done in 2014 for lesbian, gay, bisexual and transgender people (LGBT) to reach equal treatment under the law in the United States.

This year's edition emphasizes that, despite the tremendous progress in the last few years, the job is not done yet and is a call to continue the battle for full LGBT equality across the United States.

The *Gay Agenda 2014* is the most comprehensive guidebook for achieving LGBT equality and makes a timely call for action.

Part I describes what LGBT means and the arguments used to deny equal treatment under the law to this group of people.

Part II shows what the gay agenda is in detail, including the goals to be achieved.

Part III describes the different paths available to achieve equality.

Part IV details specific actions you can take in 2014 to achieve legal equality for the LGBT community.

Finally, the epilogue describes the ultimate goal—beyond legal equality.

What We Accomplished in 2013

Two important decisions of the Supreme Court in June 2013 paved the way for significant advances in legal equality for lesbian, gay, bisexual, and transgender (LGBT) Americans. Here are the main advances of 2013:

- The Supreme Court ruled that the plaintiffs appealing the California marriage case did not have standing, in effect allowing same-gender marriages to resume for good in the largest state. This meant that an additional 12% of the US population was granted the right to marry the person they love.

- In a second decision, the Supreme Court also required the federal government to recognize all legal marriages performed by a state. As a result, the Obama administration took swift action giving all 1,138 rights and obligations of marriage to all couples who live in a state where same-gender marriage is legal. For couples in other states, the administration gave as many rights as allowed by current federal law, including sponsoring the spouse for immigration, benefits to service members, and the right to file federal taxes as a married couple. However, social security benefits are still not available to same-gender couples who live in a discriminatory state, although the administration is studying whether there are alternatives.

- A record of eight states added the freedom to marry in 2013, in addition to Utah which is under appeal. From a total of nine states and the District of Columbia in 2012 to seventeen states and DC in 2013. Once the new law takes effect in Illinois (in June 2014), thirty-eight percent of the American population will live in a state with marriage equality. Five states added the freedom to marry through their legislatures: Rhode Island, Delaware, Minnesota, Illinois, and Hawai'i. Three states added it through the courts: California, New Jersey, and New Mexico. In addition, a federal district court allowed same-gender couples to marry in Utah; this decision is now under appeal.

- The Employment Non-Discrimination Act (ENDA) passed the US Senate in November 2013, but the Republican speaker of the House has not brought it up for a vote, although expectations are that if House members are allowed to vote their conscience instead of the party line, it would have a majority.

- In November 2013, Congressman Michael Michaud (D-ME) came out as gay. He became the seventh member of the current US House of Representatives who is openly lesbian, gay, or bisexual (but none is transgender). There is only one member of the US Senate who is openly LGBT, Tammy Baldwin (D-WI).

- As of 2012, there were only two states (Connecticut and Vermont) who offered total legal equality for its LGBT citizens. In 2013 two more states (California and New Jersey) and the District of Columbia where added to the list of states offering full equality. This brings it to 16% of the American population living in a state with full legal equality for its LGBT citizens.

- Colorado upgraded its domestic reciprocal beneficiaries act to civil unions and Oregon now recognizes same-gender marriages performed in other states and foreign countries (in both states, marriage equality is forbidden by a constitutional amendment).

- In Delaware, the Democratic governor signed into law marriage equality and legislation to add gender identity to its non discrimination and hate crimes statutes.

- In Nevada, the Republican governor signed into law legislation that added gender identity to its hate crimes statute.

- The Washington DC council unanimously passed the JaParker Deoni Jones Birth Certificate Amendment Act, considered by many as the model bill in the United States for equal treatment of transgender people regarding their birth certificates.

- President Obama appointed five gay men as ambassadors: John Berry to Australia, Rufus Gifford to Denmark, James

Costos to Spain, James "Wally" Brewster to the Dominican Republic, and Daniel Baer to the Organization for Security and Cooperation in Europe. He also appointed Todd Hughes to the US Court of Appeals, the first gay man appointed to such position.

- After four decades, Exodus International accepted that sexual orientation cannot be changed and shut down its operations. This organization had worked to change sexual orientation through prayer and so-called reparative therapies.

What We Accomplished in 2012

In the *Gay Agenda 2013*, we highlighted the significant advances for LGBT equality in 2012:

- President Obama came out in favor of the freedom to marry the person you love.

- LGBT voters voted 76 percent for Obama versus 22 percent for Romney. This disparity, with the support of other minority voters, gave Obama the victory in states like Florida and Ohio.

- The people of Maryland voted to allow same-gender couples to get married.

- The people of Washington State voted for the same right for its residents.

- So did the people in Maine, for a total of nine states plus the District of Columbia that currently support same-gender marriage.

- The people of Minnesota voted down a constitutional amendment that would have enshrined discrimination in their state constitution by limiting marriage to different-gender couples. In an unprecedented win, the four ballot initiatives regarding marriage were won by the supporters of equality.

- The people of Wisconsin elected Tammy Baldwin to the US Senate, the first openly LGBT person in that position.

- The people of Colorado, Rhode Island, Arizona, New York, California, and Wisconsin elected openly LGB people to represent them in the US House of Representatives. With a total of six LGB representatives, this is an all-time record. For the first time, an openly bisexual person, Kyrsten Sinema was elected to Congress representing Arizona—alas, no transgender member of Congress yet.

- For the first time in seven state legislatures, the people elected an openly LGBT person to represent them. In addition, the Washington senate elected Ed Murray (who is openly gay) as its majority leader. Moreover, the Colorado House of Representatives elected Mark Ferrandino (who is openly gay) as its speaker, and Oregon's House voted Tine Kotek (who is openly lesbian) as its speaker. They joined Gordon Fox, who has been the openly gay speaker of Rhode Island's House of Representatives since 2010.

- The Equal Employment Opportunity Commission ruled unanimously that transgender people are protected against employment discrimination under Title VII of the Civil Rights Act. Several other court rulings and agency rulings advanced employment nondiscrimination for transgender people, including protection under the Fourteenth Amendment to the US Constitution.

- Finally, in December 2012, the American Psychiatric Association removed gender identity disorder as a mental disease.

These unprecedented victories provide great momentum for a full-out action to finally achieve LGBT equality now.

Part I:

Who Are These LGBT People?

1.

Who Are These Lesbian, Gay, Bisexual, and Transgender (LGBT) People?

They are your neighbors, your coworkers, your elected officials (even if you may not realize it), your children or grandchildren (even if they do not know it yet). They are a small part of the population, but they are everywhere—in every culture, religion, location, and profession. Some live as couples, some as singles, and some are married to somebody of the opposite gender. What they all have in common is that their sexual orientation or gender identity or how they express their gender is different from the majority.

Some are exclusively attracted to members of the same gender. Others are attracted to both genders. Others feel that their anatomical gender of birth does not correspond to the gender their minds tell them they belong to. We call these people *LGBT* as the abbreviation for *lesbian, gay, bisexual, and transgender*.

Other people prefer to call themselves *queer*, which is an all-encompassing term for anybody who does not want to be classified as heterosexual or gay or lesbian or bisexual or transgender. So, sometimes the term LGBTQ is also used to include *queer*. Also, the *Q* in LGBTQ can also mean questioning, to represent people who are questioning their heterosexuality.

There are also people who are intersex, meaning that, from birth, they have both male and female genital characteristics. So another term in use is LGBTQIA for *lesbian, gay, bisexual, transexual, queer or questioning, intersex, and ally*.

There is also the term *two spirits*, used by Native Americans. Several books have been written on the topic.

Here is another, more recent term: *metrosexual*. It describes mostly men who are hip, cool, and fashionable. They are very comfortable with people of a different sexual orientation and gender identity. Metrosexuals themselves can be of any sexual orientation or gender identity or expression, although most are heterosexual.

By now, you may think that this book is *not* for you, since you may be more interested in issues such as:

- Why can't everybody just get along, marry somebody of the opposite sex, have children, and be productive members of society?

- What type of a country are we building in the United States if we allow the collapse of the traditional family?

- What will happen if we abandon our bedrock principles of individuality, respect for religion, separation of religion from state, and separation of powers in the three government branches?

This book answers these important questions. To have an opinion is easy; to learn the facts and be open to modifying our opinions based on new information is harder. Hopefully, you are willing to read here about other points of view that, you may be surprised to discover, are closer to your opinions than you may think.

Let's start with some fundamentals.

The gay agenda is not only about lesbian, gay, bisexual, and transgender people (LGBT). It is about *every person* because each of us has a sexual orientation and a gender identity and expression. As uncomfortable as the topic may be to some people, it is a very important component of who we are as people. Notice that sexual orientation refers to heterosexuality, homosexuality, and bisexuality. So laws and rules that apply to sexual orientation protect *every* person, *including heterosexuals.*

The American Psychological Association defines sexual orientation as follows:
(www.apa.org/helpcenter/sexual-orientation.aspx)

> Sexual orientation refers to an enduring pattern of emotional, romantic, and/or sexual attractions to men, women, or both sexes. Sexual orientation also refers to a person's sense of identity based on those attractions, related behaviors, and membership in a community of others who share those attractions.

Besides sexual orientation, we need to understand gender identity and expression, which is defined by the American Psychological Association as follows: (www.apa.org/topics/sexuality/transgender.aspx)

> Gender identity refers to a person's internal sense of being male, female, or something else; gender expression refers to the way a person communicates gender identity to others through behavior, clothing, hairstyles, voice, or body characteristics.

Like sexual orientation, gender identity affects every person. Most people feel comfortable that their gender at birth matches the gender that they feel they belong to; but some people feel differently. Some like to cross-dress, which is independent of sexual orientation (most cross-dressers are heterosexual—many in happy marriages). Others feel that they need to change their gender to the one they feel is their true gender.

Note that sexual orientation (the people to whom you are attracted) is different from gender identity (the gender to which you belong in your mind) and different from the expression of that gender. For instance, a male may have surgery to become a female (her gender identity is female) but at the same time be attracted to males (so her sexual orientation is heterosexual). In another example, a heterosexual female may like to dress manlier, so her gender expression may be that of a man despite that she is a heterosexual female. All the potential combinations can be mind-boggling the first time you hear about them, but life is complex and not just black and white.

For whatever reasons, some people cannot comprehend why transgender people need to change the gender of birth. However, America has a proud tradition of commitment to freedom, happiness, and individuality, so respect for others' freedom, especially about private personal matters, will eventually prevail.

Before we continue with the rest of the book, it is very important to understand that people who are gay or lesbian or bisexual or transgender are not weirdos; actually, many of them have made very important contributions to society (see a list in Appendix 1).

The next chapter talks about everyday life.

2.

A Day in the Life of a Family

The alarm goes off. It is 6:00 a.m. It seems that the alarm always goes off too early.

Lisa drags herself out of bed. She barely makes it to the kitchen, where the coffee is already brewing. Ah! What technology can do! You set it up the night before, and coffee is ready when you wake up.

Thanks to the coffee, Lisa makes it to the shower then wakes up the kids and prepares breakfast.

Mornings are always such a struggle. It is never easy with four children: Michael, Danielle, David, and Katie. Rush, rush, and rush. Lisa takes the kids to the school bus. Today is going to be a tough day. Katie, the youngest of the couple's children, is home with the flu.

The couple adopted their four children. Nobody wanted these children because they all have special needs: drug exposure during pregnancy or HIV exposure in the womb or development delays. They are great kids, but, through no fault of their own, they were rejected by other adoptive parents. Fortunately, the two kids who were exposed to HIV in the womb have tested negative. Things are going well.

The rest of the morning flies by with going to the supermarket, taking care of Katie, and doing three loads of laundry.

In the afternoon, Lisa takes the kids to after-school activities. Lisa is a very busy stay-at-home mom. She teaches the first communion classes in her church. She is also the volunteer coordinator for her children's elementary school. And she also started two Girl Scout troops.

She is the supermom that even teenagers are proud of.

Lisa rushes home to prepare dinner. Just after 7:00 p.m., Janice, her partner of eighteen years, gets home. She is exhausted after a full day of work as a manager of a state child welfare program. She is well respected for her work and knowledge (with a master's in public administration and a master's in social work).

The conversation at the dinner table centers on the children. It always does. Lisa and Janice ask them how their day at school was, review their homework, and so on—the usual stuff.

By midnight, they both have fallen asleep on the couch, pretending to watch TV.

They feel blessed for what they have. Tomorrow surely the alarm will go off again at 6:00 a.m.

For these two moms, life is not different from that of any other couple with children.

Or so they thought.

3.

A Bad Day in the Life of a Family

Lisa and Janice—along with their three youngest children, Danielle, David, and Katie—flew from rainy western Washington to sunny Florida to board a family cruise to the Bahamas to celebrate the couple's anniversary.

This was a trip that the children (and their parents) had so much looked forward to. They were in line early to board the ship. They had lunch together just after 1:00 p.m. Everyone was excited about relaxing together as a family for an entire week. What a great adventure awaited them!

After lunch, the children asked impatiently to explore the ship and headed to the top deck, where they found a basketball court. A court on a cruise ship—what could be cooler?

Janice said she was going to unpack and take a siesta (nothing like taking on a Latin tradition while in Miami). The ship wasn't scheduled to depart until 3:00 p.m., so there was plenty of time before the sail-away party.

Lisa, never one to sit still, joined the children on the top deck with her coffee in one hand and a camera in the other, not different from what any mother would do. It was such a happy day.

While taking pictures of the children, Lisa suddenly collapsed on the basketball court, spilling her coffee and dropping the camera. The children, just nine years to twelve years old, helped pick up their mom and navigated their way down ten decks to find their cabin to bang on the door and wake up their other mom, Janice.

With the help of Janice, they flagged down a porter to get a wheelchair since Lisa was unable to stand on her own. The family headed immediately to the medical center onboard. The doctor established that Lisa was gravely ill. He then requested the ship's captain to dclay departure and ordered an urgent transfer to the trauma center in Miami at Jackson Memorial Hospital. Medics arrived to take over emergency care of Lisa while a sheriff's deputy escorted Janice, the children, and their luggage to a waiting taxi. The taxi and medics carrying Lisa arrived at Ryder Trauma Center almost simultaneously around three-thirty in the afternoon.

Janice attempted to follow the gurney carrying Lisa through the emergency entrance but was asked to go to the waiting room and speak with the clerk. Janice settled the children in some chairs and headed to the desk to speak with the clerk. She asked to fill out admitting papers for Lisa, her partner, but was told to "take a seat" and wait for someone to come speak with her.

Some time later, a man appeared and introduced himself as Garnett Frederick, a hospital social worker. He then informed Janice that she and her family were in an "antigay city and state," and that if Janice wanted to find out about Lisa's condition or even see her, she needed a healthcare proxy. He turned to leave, but Janice immediately asked for his fax number and informed him that he would get the documents.

Do you know of any couple who travels with a healthcare proxy? If Janice and Lisa were a man and a woman, would anybody have asked for any documents? Would anybody have to ask, even if the couple were not married, to be allowed in the room with each other?

Janice and Lisa had their healthcare power of attorney, living wills, and advanced directives documents drawn up in 2001, shortly after Janice was diagnosed with multiple sclerosis. They tucked the documents away, never envisioning they would need them until they were much older. On that day, Lisa was only thirty-nine years old. Janice, a trained trauma and emergency department social worker, ensured that the couple kept their healthcare proxy and decision-making documents up to date.

Janice wondered in that moment at Ryder Trauma center why their love and commitment of eighteen years was not recognized. With no time to think about such injustice, she jumped into action and called a trusted friend, who rushed to the couple's house, faxed the decision-making documents to Ryder Trauma Center, and called Janice just after 4:20 p.m. to check that the fax was received at the hospital—just forty minutes after Lisa's arrival from the ship.

All of Janice's pleas to find out Lisa's condition or to speak to medical personnel went unanswered despite that the hospital had received the healthcare power of attorney. Janice watched as other families, some with young children, were escorted back through locked doors to see their loved ones while Janice's and their children's anguish increased with every minute that passed.

With papers in hand, Janice would be informed, one would think, of Lisa's medical condition, even in an antigay city and state. At 6:00 p.m.—two and half hours after their arrival—Janice was faced with a decision that would change their family forever. Surgeons informed her that Lisa was nearly brain dead and they needed to know if they should proceed with surgery. Even if Lisa survived the surgery, she would live in a persistent vegetative state. Without even seeing her, Janice was forced to make the decision to follow Lisa's wishes of donating her organs. After the surgeons left, Janice was alone to tell the children that their other mom was going to heaven.

Over the next five and a half hours, Janice begged and pleaded to see Lisa and bring their children to the room to say goodbye. She resorted to showing the children's birth certificates, which listed both of them as mothers, to the desk clerk in an attempt to establish that the children were in fact Lisa's children. They were still not allowed to see their mother.

Janice requested a Catholic priest to administer Lisa's last rites. It was only then that she was given one opportunity to see Lisa for only five minutes.

After 11:30 p.m., when Janice and the children had waited eight hours in the hospital waiting room, Lisa's sister arrived after driving from her home in Jacksonville, Florida. Janice led Lisa's sister inside and brought her to the same desk clerk who worked there all night. Lisa's sister simply stated, "I'm Lisa Pond's sister, and I am here to see her." She was informed that Lisa was moved an hour earlier to the neuro ICU and was given the room number. Lisa's sister was not asked for identification or any paperwork proving her family relationship.

Lisa Pond died of a brain aneurysm at age thirty-nine on February 19, 2007, in Jackson Memorial Hospital. Her children and the love of her life, Janice Langbehn, were a few feet away—but in another room without being able to be with Lisa in her final moments.

Without being able to touch her. Without being able to kiss her goodbye. Without being able to say, "I love you" for the final time.

This is a true story. All the information is factual. That this cruel story happened in Miami, a city that has prospered from gay tourism, tells you that it can happen anywhere.

Janice Langbehn sued the hospital. The judge dismissed the case, despite stating that the hospital "exhibited a lack of compassion and was unbecoming of a renowned trauma center like Ryder [Jackson Memorial Hospital Trauma Center]. Unfortunately, no relief is available for these failures based on the allegations pleaded in the amended complaint."

In other words, there was nothing to sue about because no law had been broken. Hospital visitation discrimination like this was allowed in Florida and other states until January 18, 2011, when new regulations came into effect at the urging of President Obama after learning of the Langbehn-Pond story.

Lisa and Janice, together for eighteen years, parents of four children whom nobody else wanted, were cruelly denied a basic human need: to have your loved ones next to you when you die. In Janice's words, "Holding Lisa's hand is not a *gay* right but a *human* right."

4.

Your Family's Values

Family is very personal, and how you raise your family is up to you. As a father and mother said: "We don't want others to impose *their* family values on our family."

It is all about *your family's* values. For example, this father and mother's family values are clear: they have two daughters, Jackie and Debbie. One daughter is lesbian; the other is not. Taking turns, the parents both said, "Our family's values are that we treat our two daughters the same. We teach them the same ethics and values. We want them to have the same opportunities. We want them to be happy in their lives and one day to marry someone they love and start their own families. We treat our two daughters equally and expect the government to do the same. These are our family's values."

One day recently, this family found out that they held a prejudice that they had not previously realized. They encouraged their non-lesbian daughter, Jackie, to bring her boyfriend home for dinner (but not stay overnight) to ensure that he could get to know the family and vice versa. However, they were uncomfortable asking Debbie to bring her girlfriend.

The parents said: "We did not realize that we were treating our two daughters differently and that we could cause harm that way. Now we check everything we do as parents, to show both our daughters that we love them equally and unconditionally. And it is fine for our daughter Debbie to bring her girlfriend for dinner and family outings—but neither of our daughters gets to bring a boyfriend or girlfriend overnight." The parents and daughters laughed together as they recounted the story.

What this father and mother are doing is very good parenting. Scientific research by the Family Acceptance Project of San Francisco State University (familyproject.sfsu.edu) shows the following:

- Suicide attempts by LGBT youth who have high rejection from their family are more than *eight times* the attempts in families with low rejection for their LGBT children.

- Illegal drug use by LGBT youth who experience high rejection from their family is more than *three times* the use for those in families with low rejection for their LGBT children.

- Similarly, the risk of HIV infection is more than *three times* for LGBT youth in families with a high rejection for them.

- Yet another important statistic: 92 percent of LGBT youth in a family that is highly accepting believe that they can be a happy LGBT adult, while only 35 percent of those in a family that is not accepting believe it so.

Several religious leaders are working with the Family Acceptance Project because these scientific findings have opened their minds that tough love can be very detrimental to the health (and survival) of young LGBT people.

Each person is entitled to his or her faith. You may believe that LGBT people will not go to heaven. Other people believe in an all-loving God and that a good person (whether gay or non-gay) will go to heaven. Every parent knows that *love for a child must be unconditional*, in good times and in bad.

There are several parental behaviors that increase the risk of LGBT children developing health and mental problems. These parental behaviors are determined to be unhealthy based not on opinion but on scientific research by the Family Acceptance Project (familyproject.sfsu.edu). Here are nine behaviors to avoid:

1. "Hitting, slapping or physically hurting your child because of their LGBT identity."

2. "Verbal harassment or name-calling because of your child's LGBT identity."

3. "Excluding LGBT youth from family and family identity."

4. "Blocking access to LGBT friends, events and resources."

5. "Blaming your child when they are discriminated against because of their LGBT identity."

6. "Pressuring your child to be more (or less) masculine or feminine."

7. "Telling your children that God will punish them because they are gay."

8. "Telling your child that you are ashamed of them or that how they look or act will shame the family."

9. "Making your child keep their LGBT identity a secret in the family and not letting them talk about it."

All parents want the best for their children. When parents decide what's best for their children, they draw on experiences with their parents (good or bad) and all the other experiences from which they have learned throughout their lives. However, most parents have no experience dealing with LGBT children; so, they may respond based on ideas of tough love instead of responses proven to work. Fortunately, research conducted by the Family Acceptance Project shows parental behaviors that can be most helpful to their LGBT children. These recommendations are not based on opinions or beliefs, but on research. Here are eleven things to do:

1. "Talk with your child or foster child about their LGBT identity."

2. "Express affection when your child tells you or when you learn that your child is gay or transgender."

3. "Support your child's LGBT identity even though you may feel uncomfortable."

4. "Advocate for your child when he or she is mistreated because of their LGBT identity."

5. "Require that other family members respect your LGBT child."

6. "Bring your child to LGBT organizations or events."

7. "Talk with your clergy and help your faith community to support LGBT people."

8. "Connect your child with an LGBT adult role model to show them options for the future."

9. "Welcome your child's LGBT friends and partners to your home."

10. "Support your child's gender expression."

11. "Believe your child can have a happy future as an LGBT adult."

This scientific research is opening up many minds—teaching parents to understand the unintended consequences of their past behavior.

For religious parents, this may appear like a conflict, especially when some churches say that homosexuality is an abomination. However, more and more religious leaders are reaching out after understanding the science—and more and more Christian parents accept what Jesus has always taught: *unconditional love and commitment*, which is the basis of marriage and of having children. Good parents always want to protect their children from harm.

If you are conflicted about loving your child because he is LGBT, read the blog www.JustBecauseHeBreathes.com written by two conservative evangelical parents. Do not miss the letter from the father to his gay son, Ryan. Also, watch the videos by the Family Acceptance Project: FamilyProject.sfsu.edu/family-videos

In summary, you decide your family's values.

What, then, is the definition of a family?

5.

Defining *Family*

In the last few chapters we have met two families: one a non-traditional but sanctified union, the other with more traditional parents but daughters of different sexual orientations.

How *does* one then define a family? Traditionalists have a clear answer: mother + father + children. This is *their* definition of family. What's *your* definition for *your* family?

As an example, here is the definition that Baptist Health South Florida has for a family (in their 2011 *Outcomes*—a compilation of articles from their Center for Performance Excellence):

> The word *family* triggers images of different "support groups" for each of us. Over time, the "social support group" to us changes, shifts, or expands throughout our lives.
>
> At Baptist Health, each patient defines those individuals who are most important to them—who they view as "family." We recognize and value the importance of these individuals in the healing process. These people may include, but are not limited to, family, friends, and/or other support persons, such as a spouse, a domestic partner (including same-sex domestic partner), other relatives, neighbors, coworkers or clergy. **In other words, each patient has the right to define who can be present and participate in their care and visitation.**

The bold typeface is in the original article. Note that Baptist Health South Florida is a *faith-based* healthcare organization ranking at the top in the United States. They understand the definition of a family since they see patients constantly defining who their families are.

There is an account of other families in the book *Ties that Bind* by Isay Dave.

Each of us knows who our true family is: the people we turn to when we are most in need. How have we come to allow others to impose a definition of who should be our families?

This is an attack on our personal freedom.

People use several arguments to deny others' freedoms. Let's examine these arguments one by one in the next chapters.

6.

It's Unnatural!

Some people think that homosexual, bisexual, and transgender people are mentally sick, that what they do is unnatural, and that the Bible says it is an abomination. These beliefs serve as a justification for people to discriminate, such as to deny a family the right to be together when the mother was dying at a hospital, as we saw in Chapter 3.

Would God accept the behavior of the people in that hospital in Miami who did not allow Lisa's partner to be next to her as she was dying? What about their young children, who had nothing to do with their parents' sexual orientation?

Let's discuss now one of the most common arguments used to discriminate: that homosexuality is a sin against nature.

To see if it is true, we need to check whether homosexuality and bisexuality exist in animals in nature.

Evidence is very clear that many animals exhibit homosexual and bisexual behaviors. Here are just a few examples from Wikipedia: (en.wikipedia.org/wiki/Homosexual_behavior_in_animals)

- *Giraffes:* about nine out of ten matings occur between males.

- *Domesticated sheep:* about 10 percent of males do not mate with females—only males.

- *Black swans:* about 25 percent of the matings are between males. Male couples also raise young black swans.

- *Western gulls:* 10 to 15 percent of females show homosexual behavior.

- *Wild ducks:* about 19 percent of all pairings are male with male.

- *Penguins:* many male-to-male long-term relationships have been reported, including building nests together.

- *Vultures:* bisexual vultures have been studied in zoos.

- *Pigeons:* male-male and female-female relationships have been documented. Same-gender couples build nests together.

- *American bisons:* same-sex relationships are documented as common.

- *Bonobos (apes):* they are considered a bisexual species (60 percent of sexual activity is between two or more females).

- *Dolphins:* there is well-reported bisexual behavior, especially among bottlenose dolphins.

- *Elephants:* there is well-documented bisexual behavior, with stronger bonds between males.

- *Lions:* about 8 percent of mountings are male-male.

- *Spotted hyena:* have strong female-to-female relationships.

- *Lizards:* females can take masculine or feminine sexual roles.

- *Dragonflies:* high incidence of mating among males.

This article concludes, *"No species has been found in which homosexual behavior has not been shown to exist, except for species that never have sex at all."* Therefore, we cannot say that homosexuality and bisexuality are unnatural when they have been well-documented in nature.

Some people would say, "Fine, we cannot say that it is unnatural, but these people are mentally sick." The next chapter responds to this pronouncement.

7.

You Are Sick!

Given the scientific evidence, we need to agree that homosexuality and bisexuality occur naturally in animals. What about in humans? Has this topic been studied by science? The answer is yes. Research by psychologists like Alfred Kinsey, Magnus Hirschfeld, and Sigmund Freud, among others, shows that sexual orientation appears as a spectrum from totally heterosexual to bisexual to totally homosexual.

Repeated studies show that people fall into different parts of the spectrum of sexual orientation. This is a natural phenomenon. For example, handedness falls also into a continuous spectrum: most people are right-handed, some are left-handed, and some are ambidextrous.

The American Psychological Association confirms: (www.apa.org/helpcenter/sexual-orientation.aspx)

> Both heterosexual behavior and homosexual behavior are normal aspects of human sexuality. Both have been documented in many different cultures and historical eras. Despite the persistence of stereotypes that portray lesbian, gay, and bisexual people as disturbed, several decades of research and clinical experience have led all mainstream medical and mental health organizations in this country to conclude that these orientations represent normal forms of human experience. Lesbian, gay, and bisexual relationships are normal forms of human bonding. Therefore, these mainstream organizations long ago abandoned classifications of homosexuality as a mental disorder.

Clearly, scientific organizations have concluded that homosexuality, heterosexuality, and bisexuality are normal forms of the human experience and that they are not mental disorders.

We cannot say that homosexuality is unnatural since it occurs in nature. Furthermore, we cannot say that people with a homosexual sexual orientation are sick since it has been proven scientifically not to be the case.

But, you may say, the Bible says homosexuality is an abomination. You are right on this one—read on.

8.

The Bible Says So

We have already seen that we cannot call homosexuality unnatural since it is well-documented that it happens in nature. Nor can we say that homosexuality is a disease since for several decades the American Psychological Association and other organizations have clearly stated that it is a normal aspect of human sexuality.

So, it's not unnatural, and it is not a disease. However, some people believe that, based on what the Bible says, homosexuality is an abomination.

Indeed, Leviticus 18:22 (King James Version) clearly says, "Thou shalt not lie with mankind, as with womankind: it is an abomination." Some experts contend that the term *abomination* is mistranslated. But since religion is based on personal faith, we should respect those who take the meaning literally.

Furthermore, Leviticus 20:13 (King James Version) establishes the death penalty for homosexual acts:

> If a man also lie with mankind, as he lieth with a woman, both of them have committed an abomination: they shall surely be put to death; their blood shall be upon them.

If you are willing to accept that homosexual acts are an abomination subject to the death penalty then you have to accept the penalty that the same chapter of Leviticus establishes:

> **Leviticus 20:9** For every one that curseth his father or his mother shall be surely put to death: he hath cursed his father or his mother; his blood shall be upon him.

> **Leviticus 20:10** And the man that committeth adultery with another man's wife, even he that committeth adultery with his neighbour's wife, the

adulterer and the adulteress shall surely be put to death.

Leviticus 20:11 And the man that lieth with his father's wife hath uncovered his father's nakedness: both of them shall surely be put to death; their blood shall be upon them.

Leviticus 20:12 And if a man lie with his daughter in law, both of them shall surely be put to death: they have wrought confusion; their blood shall be upon them.

Leviticus 20:13 If a man also lie with mankind, as he lieth with a woman, both of them have committed an abomination: they shall surely be put to death; their blood shall be upon them.

Leviticus 20:14 And if a man take a wife and her mother, it is wickedness: they shall be burnt with fire, both he and they; that there be no wickedness among you.

Leviticus 20:15 And if a man lie with a beast, he shall surely be put to death: and ye shall slay the beast.

Leviticus 20:16 And if a woman approach unto any beast, and lie down thereto, thou shalt kill the woman, and the beast: they shall surely be put to death; their blood shall be upon them.

Leviticus 20:17 And if a man shall take his sister, his father's daughter, or his mother's daughter, and see her nakedness, and she see his nakedness; it is a wicked thing; and they shall be cut off in the sight of their people: he hath uncovered his sister's nakedness; he shall bear his iniquity.

Leviticus 20:18 And if a man shall lie with a woman having her sickness, and shall uncover her nakedness; he hath discovered her fountain, and she hath uncovered the fountain of her blood: and both of them shall be cut off from among their people.

Leviticus 20:19 And thou shalt not uncover the nakedness of thy mother's sister, nor of thy father's sister: for he uncovereth his near kin: they shall bear their iniquity.

Leviticus 20:20 And if a man shall lie with his uncle's wife, he hath uncovered his uncle's nakedness: they shall bear their sin; they shall die childless.

Leviticus 20:21 And if a man shall take his brother's wife, it is an unclean thing: he hath uncovered his brother's nakedness; they shall be childless.

So if you curse your father or mother, you should be put to death. And if you commit adultery with a married woman, both of you should be put to death. So if you believe that homosexual acts are an abomination that results in the perpetrators deserving to be put to death then you should be consistent with the other commandments in the same chapter of Leviticus. There are more commandments in Leviticus:

Leviticus 11:10–12 And all that have not fins and scales in the seas, and in the rivers, of all that move in the waters, and of any living thing which is in the waters, they shall be an abomination unto you. They shall be even an abomination unto you; ye shall not eat of their flesh, but ye shall have their carcasses in abomination. Whatsoever hath no fins nor scales in the waters, that shall be an abomination unto you.

So, not only are homosexual acts an abomination but eating shrimp and other fish without fins is an abomination, too. The point is not to debate or contest *your* interpretation of the Bible. Some Christians believe that the translation may not consider the context of the times and the exact meaning of the words. Other Christians believe that the Bible should be read literally; if this is your belief, please act consistently by choosing what you cannot eat and lobby to establish the death penalty not only for homosexual acts but also for the heterosexual acts listed in Leviticus. The point here is not to change your religious beliefs but to encourage you to be *consistent* with them. In fact, it is very important to respect and protect the freedom of religion, as the next chapter attests.

9.

Your Freedom of Religion

"A gay person who is seeking God, who is of good
will—well, who am I to judge him."

—Pope Francis, July 28, 2013

Clearly, in a civilized society, we are not going to execute men who commit adultery with married women, just as we are not going to execute people who have romantic relationships with a person of the same gender. Similarly, in a civilized society, we are not going to call people with a homosexual sexual orientation an abomination but remain silent about people who commit the abomination, per Leviticus 11, of eating shrimp or any shellfish.

Fortunately, most Americans want to respect each other's freedom of religion. It is true: some religions do believe that homosexual acts should be penalized and that indeed people with a homosexual sexual orientation should not be treated equally under the law. However, some other religions differ; they believe that every person is a child of God, loved by God, and should be treated equally.

Some people, however, work hard to attack the freedom of religion. In January 2013, the National Cathedral, which is the second largest church in the United States and part of the Episcopal faith, announced that it will marry people of the same gender. A month after that decision, the Faith and Freedom Coalition, an organization founded by conservative Ralph Reed, demanded "an immediate suspension of any current or future federal funds to this institution." So much for their belief in freedom of religion.

How do we go about protecting freedom of religion?

We should protect the freedom of each religion, since we can only protect your freedom of religion if we protect others' freedom of religion. If your religion believes that homosexuality is an abomination and does not allow people of the same gender to marry, it is fine. If your religion accepts people with a homosexual sexual orientation and their right to marry, fine, too. The government should not impose on any religion whom to marry (or divorce) or force any religion to have bishops who are female or LGBT.

Government cannot impose one religion's views on another. This is why each religion is regulated by its own laws and civic life by its own laws. Americans cherish the requirement expressed in the United States Constitution:

> Congress shall make no law respecting an establishment of religion, or prohibiting the free exercise thereoff.

The greatness of our country comes from not allowing Sharia law to control all of us. Nor do we allow Jewish law, or Catholic law, or Baptist law to control all of us. Every individual is free to follow the law of his or her church, while the government creates and enforces civil law.

The New Mexico Supreme Court said it eloquently in their marriage equality decision on December 19, 2013: "Our analysis does not and cannot depend on religious doctrine without violating the Constitution."

Still, some people say that our *civil* laws should not treat people with a homosexual sexual orientation equally because homosexuality is a choice. But is it a choice? The next chapter tackles this important question.

10.

Is Homosexuality a Choice?

Sexual orientation defines our attraction to other people. By definition, sexual orientation can be heterosexual (attracted to people of a different gender), homosexual (attracted to people of the same gender), or bisexual (attracted to people of either gender).

So the question is: is sexual orientation a choice?

Ask this question to yourself. Is *your* sexual orientation a choice? If you answer yes, when did you choose your sexual orientation? How did you make that choice?

Or, more pointedly, for heterosexuals: when did you decide to be a heterosexual? Did you decide you were heterosexual even before you had sex? Did you always know because you were just born that way? Did it just come naturally?

Certainly, most readers have answered no—meaning that sexual orientation was not a choice for them. Bisexual individuals may answer that at some point they were attracted to one gender and at some other point in their lives to the other or that they were equally attracted to both.

If your child tells you that he or she is gay or lesbian or bisexual or transgender, do not blame yourself. *You did nothing wrong.* You did not influence him or her to be LGBT, nor did your parents influence you to be a heterosexual, just as homosexual parents cannot influence their children to be LGBT. It is the way it is. There is growing research that the sexual orientation of the parents—heterosexual, homosexual, or bisexual—does not affect the orientation of the children they raise.

The people who believe that homosexuality is a choice use this to deny people with a different sexual orientation or gender identity equal protection under the law. They claim that the law should protect all citizens equally regardless of race, gender, or national origin because those factors are obviously not a choice.

Here is the catch: while the law protects against discrimination based on non-choice characteristics such as race, gender, and national origin, it also protects *religion*—which is clearly a personal choice. So you cannot fairly say that it is okay to discriminate against gays because being gay is a choice. Even if homosexuality were a choice, it should be protected against discrimination.

There is yet another argument that some people still use to justify discrimination against gay, lesbian, bisexual, and transgender people. They say it can be cured. Let's consider this question in the next chapter.

11.

Let *Me* Straighten *You*

If your sexual orientation is heterosexual, do you think that with therapy you could become homosexual?

You are very likely to answer: *"No way. Nobody would be able to make me homosexual. And I do not want to change anyway."*

Indeed, most people do not want to change something as intrinsic as their sexual orientation, whether they are heterosexual, homosexual, or bisexual.

However, there is heavy societal pressure to belong to the majority. So whether because of their religion, or not knowing that sexual orientation falls naturally into a spectrum, or fear of rejection by society, some people still struggle with their sexual orientation. They try to change their sexual orientation to heterosexual and "be cured." Some families, for similar reasons, bring their children to therapy (called reparative or conversion therapy) to "make them straight."

As hard as it might be to believe for those who think that homosexuality is an abomination, there is nothing to be cured.

The most important study on the subject was conducted in 2001 by Robert Spitzer, MD, a well-respected professor of psychiatry at Columbia University. Dr. Spitzer addressed the issue of whether individuals could change their sexual orientation from homosexual to heterosexual using reparative or conversation therapy. He concluded that *some* highly motivated individuals could do it. The report was published in the *Archives of Sexual Behavior* but was not peer-reviewed, a critical requirement for any scientific work. Eventually, Dr. Spitzer concluded that his research was fundamentally flawed, and that there was no evidence that reparative therapy worked because statements from participants about their self-evaluation of the success of such therapy could not be relied upon.

This is what the American Psychological Association has to say regarding therapies to change sexual orientation: (www.apa.org/helpcenter/sexual-orientation.aspx)

> To date, there has been no scientifically adequate research to show that therapy aimed at changing sexual orientation (sometimes called reparative or conversion therapy) is safe or effective. Furthermore, it seems likely that the promotion of change therapies reinforces stereotypes and contributes to a negative climate for lesbian, gay, and bisexual persons. This appears to be especially likely for lesbian, gay, and bisexual individuals who grow up in more conservative religious settings.

So there is no evidence that such therapies are safe or effective.

The most prominent organization involved in so-called reparative or conversion therapy is Exodus International. In an interesting twist, Michael Bussee, one of its cofounders, left the organization in 1979 to live together with another cofounder of Exodus, Gary Cooper. To go even further, they had a commitment ceremony in 1982 (well before civil unions or marriage equality existed).

Years later, in October 2000, the chair of Exodus International, John Paulk, was removed from his position after being spotted drinking and flirting at a gay bar in Washington, DC.

More recently, in 2011, John Smid, the former executive director of Love in Action (another organization that claimed to "straighten homosexuals"), said, "I never met a man who experienced a change from homosexual to heterosexual."

Putting a final nail to this coffin, Alan Chambers, the president of Exodus International, said in June 2012 that "there was no cure for homosexuality and that 'reparative therapy' offered false hopes to gays and could even be harmful."

So it doesn't work.

Finally, after forty years, Exodus International closed its doors in 2013. Its president, Alan Chambers, stated:

> Exodus is an institution in the conservative Christian world, but we've ceased to be a living, breathing organism. For quite some time we've been imprisoned in a worldview that's neither honoring toward our fellow human beings, nor biblical.

On April 24, 2013, the former chair of Exodus International, John Paulk stated:

> Please allow me to be clear: I do not believe that reparative therapy changes sexual orientation; in fact, it does great harm to people.

Despite such clear statements, other organizations continue to try to straighten LGBT people. Such an organization is Courage, a Catholic apostolate. There's a twist: Paul Scalia, a priest who is the son of virulently antigay Supreme Court Justice Scalia, works there.

A very good resource and an organization worth supporting is Truth Wins Out (www.thruthwinsout.org). This organization specializes in debunking the ex-gay myth and counters disinformation campaigns about LGBT people. Its founder, Wayne Besen, is the author of *Anything but Straight: Unmasking the Scandals and Lies Behind the Ex-Gay Myth*. It is a book worth reading if you want to know more about this topic.

Some people may say, "Okay, I accept gays but please do not flaunt it." This concern is addressed in the following chapter.

12.

Don't Flaunt It

Some people say they can *tolerate* people who are gay, lesbian, bisexual, or transgender—but they add: "Just don't flaunt it." These people think that not "flaunting" sexual orientation, or hiding it, is a good compromise. In reality, this so-called compromise is harming (albeit unintentionally) LGBT people.

An important part of a healthy mind is to be able to be who you are. This was a main argument expressed by the chairman of the Joint Chiefs of Staff, Admiral Mullen, in support of the repeal of "Don't Ask, Don't Tell": it is *immoral* to force people to lie about and hide who they are.

Furthermore, a civilized society means that we respect other people—not just tolerate them. For instance, many years ago, the World Jewish Congress changed its vocabulary from "tolerance" to "respect."

It is wonderful to see a couple holding hands and showing their love. It is a public demonstration of commitment, love, and caring. It is wonderful independent of the gender of the couple. Notice that we are talking about public displays of affection—not about having sex in public (which is not appropriate whether the couple is same gender or different gender).

But what about the children? Some people say, "I do not want my children to see a homosexual couple. It is bad for the kids." Some people say that out of concern that seeing such a couple will make the child homosexual. Of course, this is not true: if you are heterosexual, can you fathom for a second that you would have become homosexual just by seeing a same-gender couple holding hands when you were a child? Let's be real.

In reality, you may be causing harm to your children if they see you reacting negatively about a same-gender couple's public display of affection. The message that you are sending is that homosexuality is wrong and that you may not love your children if they are homosexual. Seeing a same-gender public display of affection is an opportunity for you to teach the importance of understanding for, acceptance of, and respect for other human beings—and to let your children know that you will still love them even if they are homosexual or bisexual or transgender. Because you *will* still love them—won't you?

For those interested in the science, here is what the American Psychological Association has to say: (www.apa.org/helpcenter/sexual-orientation.aspx)

> Sexual orientation is commonly discussed as if it were solely a characteristic of an individual, like biological sex, gender identity, or age. This perspective is incomplete because sexual orientation is defined in terms of relationships with others. People express their sexual orientation through behaviors with others, including such simple actions as holding hands or kissing. Thus, sexual orientation is closely tied to the intimate personal relationships that meet deeply felt needs for love, attachment, and intimacy. In addition to sexual behaviors, these bonds include nonsexual physical affection between partners, shared goals and values, mutual support, and ongoing commitment. Therefore, sexual orientation is not merely a personal characteristic within an individual. Rather, one's sexual orientation defines the group of people in which one is likely to find the satisfying and fulfilling romantic relationships that are an essential component of personal identity for many people.

So, it is about flaunting it. The freedom to be yourself is a part of one's sexual orientation and gender identity and expression and is a necessary component of a healthy lifestyle. It is about the freedom and respect to be yourself and have your individuality. Some people get it—check the next chapter.

13.

Understand, Accept, and Respect

More than thirty years ago, a young man, proud of being the big man in high school, started his first day of college to discover that he had been assigned a gay roommate. He was surprised but accepted it. After their freshman year, their lives took different courses. This young man ended up on Wall Street and was by the Twin Towers on September 11, 2001. Thankfully, he survived.

Life continued, and when President Obama announced his support for the freedom to marry, this young man e-mailed his freshman roommate of more than thirty years ago:

> With the President coming out and making a statement on same sex marriage I reference you often. I speak that you and I still stay in touch after all these years and that you were the first person to contact me after 9/11. I will always remember that. I have you and your friends to thank for enabling me to understand, accept and respect gay people. Being 18 and big man on campus in HS, if you were going to tell me that my college roommate would be gay, I would have said you're crazy. Just another example of not judging a book by its cover. It's wonderful that the time we were roommates has left a lasting impact on me.

> Thanks again.

> Be well.

Understand, accept, and respect.

That's all that needs to be said.

14.

It's about Personal Freedom; It's about Being Better People

The essence of personal freedom is to live and let live. For you to be free means that others need to be free. For example, you are free to follow a religious belief that homosexuality is an abomination. But you have to let others be free to follow their own religious belief that God loves all His creatures equally, including practicing homosexuals.

However, you are not free to cause bodily or psychological harm to others.

You should not stop others from having the same rights as you do or vote against them having the same rights that you have.

So this book is about freedom, as well as being better people.

It's about respecting others' choices—giving them freedom, even if we disagree. You may not want romantic intimacy with somebody of the same gender. However, we should respect and celebrate the fact that two people love each other—even if they are the same gender.

Being better people is about knowing that we are *not judging*. It is not about tolerating others but about respecting and celebrating their freedom to be unique—maybe very different from you or from the majority but still unique individuals with their virtues and faults, like each of us.

Being a better person, being free and respecting the personal freedom of others, and being treated equally under the law are the fundamental essence that most of us who love our country share.

15.

Summary: Who Are These LGBT People?

In the preceding chapters, we have learned a little bit more about lesbian, gay, bisexual, and transgender individuals. In summary, LGBT people are not alien to our lives. They are our neighbors, paramedics, firefighters, elected officials, military personnel, writers, police officers, and others in all professions, backgrounds, and locations. They are also people who have made very important contributions to society in the military, the sciences, the arts, and many other fields. We have seen that you cannot call homosexuality or bisexuality unnatural since it happens every day in nature. Science also agrees that homosexuality is not a disease and that there is nothing to cure, nor is there any effective method to change an individual's sexual orientation.

We have also seen that although the Bible can be interpreted as saying that homosexual acts are an abomination, not everybody agrees with that interpretation. (But if you do, to be consistent you cannot commit any other abomination, such as eating shrimp.)

Freedom of religion is very important. Since different religions have different religious laws about matters such as marriage, divorce, ordination, role of women, etc., we cannot impose one religion over another when we create *civil laws*.

Further, we've learned that the issue is not whether homosexuality is a choice: religion is clearly a personal choice and is included in all of our nondiscrimination legislation (as it should be).

Finally, we've seen that family values are defined by each family. For many families, a most important value is that they want all their children to be treated equally—independent of their sexual orientation or gender identity or expression.

Now that we know who these LGBT people are, it is time to examine the gay agenda. What do lesbian, gay, bisexual, and transgender individuals want? Do they want special rights? These and other questions will be explored in the next chapters.

Part II:

Why A Gay Agenda?

16.

Special Rights

Does anyone deserve special rights?

Think about it. Commit to an answer.

My answer is this: yes, some people deserve special rights.

What?

You got it right: some people do deserve special rights. Take, for example, a married couple. They get special rights. Here are some of the special rights married couples get:

- Unlimited, tax-free transfer of assets between spouses (including at death)

- Filing taxes jointly

- Making medical decisions for each other and their children

- Survivor Social Security benefits after death of a spouse

- Funeral and bereavement leave

- Ability to file wrongful death claims

- Spousal communications privilege that protects confidential communications between spouses during civil and criminal cases

- Spousal testimonial privilege that allows spouses not to testify against each other in a court of law

- Ability to sponsor the other spouse for immigration to the United States

- Joint adoption and foster care

- Automatic legal status with stepchildren

These are just some of the 1,138 special rights that married people get (per the report of the United States General Accounting Office dated January 23, 2004). Indeed, they should get them.

There are also special rights conferred to some people as protections against discrimination or hate crimes. These special rights are based on characteristics at birth that cannot be changed, such as race, gender, and country of origin. Some of the special protections are based on characteristics that are, and should be, a personal choice, such as choice of religion.

So, LGBT people are not seeking special rights that nobody else receives—just to be treated like people in the same circumstances.

If you are not gay, why should you care about gay rights? You might be surprised by some of the reasons, discussed in the following chapter.

17.

If I Am Not Gay, Why Should I Care about Gay Rights?

Because the crucial issue is not about gay rights; it is about who we are as a country and as good human beings. Do we accept the personal freedom of others to be unique individuals? Should anybody have to fear for their lives or their jobs just for being who they are? It is all about basic human rights. It is about the fundamental belief that we all share in America to be treated equally under the law.

Also, you should care if you have young children or grandchildren. They already have a sexual orientation (heterosexual, homosexual, or bisexual), even if they are too young to know. We have already discussed that conversion therapies do not work. Wouldn't you then want for them to live in a country in which they are treated equally under the law, independent of their sexual orientation and gender identity and expression?

Here's another example: say that you are heterosexual and a great accountant who wants to work for an LGBT organization that provides great benefits and it is close to your home. You should not be discriminated against because of your sexual orientation; you should be able to work for a gay organization. Discrimination based on sexual orientation (heterosexual, homosexual, or bisexual) should not be allowed, and the same goes for gender identity (the gender you identify with) and expression (how you express your gender).

Here's one more example: imagine you are outside a public restroom holding your wife's purse. You are 100-percent heterosexual, but some thugs think that because you are holding a purse, you are homosexual, and they attack you as they shout, "Faggot! Faggot! Here is what you deserve!" This is a true story.

Nobody deserves to be a victim of a hate crime. Thanks to legislation passed by Congress and signed into law in 2009 by

President Obama, you are protected against hate crimes because of your religion, race, national origin, gender, sexual orientation, gender identity and expression, and disability.

Now that you care about equal rights for everybody, what's the gay agenda? We'll get closer to an answer in the next chapter, which describes a gay congressman's agenda.

18.

Barney Frank's Radical Homosexual Agenda

Barney Frank was, until his retirement in January 2013, the most senior openly gay member of Congress. He was a member of Congress for more than thirty years and was chair of the powerful House Financial Services Committee for four years. He was considered by many to be a very savvy legislator. He is a graduate of Harvard College and Harvard Law School.

On December 22, 2010, four days after Congress repealed "Don't Ask, Don't Tell," Representative Frank addressed, during a press conference, what others called the "Barney Frank radical homosexual agenda." He said that this agenda was:

1. To be protected against violent crimes driven by bigotry

2. To be able to get married

3. To be able to get a job

4. To be able to fight for our country

He added, "For those who are worried about the radical homosexual agenda, let me put them on notice—two down, two to go." As for the "two down," he was referring to the repeal of "Don't Ask, Don't Tell" and the expansion of federal hate-crimes legislation to include sexual orientation and gender identity and expression. The "two to go" referred to the right to get married and to employment nondiscrimination.

As much as he is respected, and as much as his speech was wonderful and punchy, this is not the gay agenda. As the next chapter discusses, we need to think bigger.

19.

Thinking *Bigger*

Congressman Frank's "two down, two to go" should be more like "one and a half down, several more to go."

The "one" that is "down" is the hate-crimes protection that was achieved (at the federal level) when President Obama signed into law the Matthew Shepard and James Byrd, Jr. Hate Crimes Prevention Act on October 28, 2009. Here's a caveat: this legislation, while very useful, is not a replacement for state hate-crimes legislation, which is really needed in each state.

A goal that is half down is for service members serving openly in the military. As we explain in Chapter 27, these service members can still be discriminated against, and transgender service members are still not allowed to serve their country.

In terms of the two to go, Congressman Frank is referring to marriage and employment nondiscrimination. However, there are more than two goals that need to be achieved, including anti-bullying and safety in the schools, parenting rights, and nondiscrimination in housing, financing, public accommodations, and federal government programs.

The LGBT movement, while making significant progress (especially in the states, courts, and public opinion), suffers from not thinking big enough. We saw that Barney Frank's "radical homosexual agenda" was incomplete. For some people, the approach is: *ask for little—get even less.*

So, what's the real gay agenda? The true gay agenda is disclosed in detail in the next chapter.

20.

Q: What's the Gay Agenda?

A: The American Agenda–
Equal Treatment under the Law

"The compelling argument is on the side of
homosexuals. That's where the compelling
argument is: 'We're Americans. We just want to be
treated like everybody else.'"

—Bill O'Reilly on Fox News, March 26, 2013

The gay agenda is very simple: being treated equally under the
law, which happens to be the American Agenda. This is the shared
belief among Americans that has made us such a great country. It
is the Golden Rule of treating others as you want to be treated.

To achieve the gay agenda, just look at the laws (federal and state)
—whenever you see protections based on race, gender, national
origin, and religion, just add the words *sexual orientation* and
gender identity.

That's it. As Harvey Milk said:

> All men are created equal. No matter how hard you
> try, you can never erase those words.

If you have read the previous chapters of this book, you know that:

- Nobody is asking for special rights. LGBT people just want
  to be treated like other groups—no need to create special
  legislation for us. Just add "sexual orientation and gender
  identity" to existing legislation.

- Nobody is comparing the suffering of different groups protected under the law. People have suffered tremendous discrimination and prejudice because of their race. People have suffered tremendous discrimination and prejudice because of their gender, and because of their national origin, and because of their religion, and because of their sexual orientation, and because of their gender identity.

- Nobody wants to curtail your freedom of religion. Some religions support LGBT equality while others oppose it. The government cannot pick one religion over another. So public policy is based on treating everybody equally under the law. Each religion has the right to decide whom to marry, whom to allow to remarry in that faith, or whom to elevate to priesthood, among other rights.

- Whether being LGBT is a choice or not is irrelevant in this discussion. Religion clearly is a personal choice, and it is (and should be) protected against discrimination. Similarly, sexual orientation and gender identity and expression should be protected, too.

So what are the areas of the law in which LGBT people are not treated equally?

- Hates crimes
- Nondiscrimination
- Military
- Marriage equality
- Freedom of gender
- Protecting youth
- Same-gender parenting

Each of these areas is an equality goal—what needs to be achieved to be treated equally under the law. Each equality goal is discussed in detail in the successive chapters.

One point to note before we continue: some people state that the real gay agenda is social justice or to be equal in real life, not just under the law. This is a very honorable objective. However, as we have seen in prior chapters, real equality comes very slowly, even after legal equality is reached. For example, forty-five years after interracial marriage was made legal in all fifty states by the

Supreme Court, some people still oppose it (a significant number of people, in some states).

For the real, long-term gay agenda, do not miss reading the epilogue of this book. The immediate focus of our energy is on legal equality under the law. How difficult is this to achieve?

21.

It's Not Rocket Science

"Discrimination is complicated.
Equality is remarkably simple."

—John Lewis,
Legal director of Marriage Equality USA

Some problems are very difficult. Launching a rocket to the moon, landing it there, and bringing the astronauts safely home is a very difficult problem. We are the only country in the world to have solved it. Overhauling the medical system in a country is a difficult problem. Treating everybody equally under the law is not a difficult problem to solve. Here is how it can be done:

1. Examine the areas of the law in which lesbian, gay, bisexual, and transgender individuals are not treated equally. Call these areas equality goals. (This is simple, yet LGBT organizations still talk about issues instead of goals—just check their websites.)

2. Create a way to measure progress at the federal level and in each of the states so you can report accurately how many goals have been achieved instead of saying, "Two down, two to go," as Representative Frank claimed.

3. Write these equality goals in legal terms. You can put it all into an omnibus bill. Whether you seek passage as one bill or as a collection of bills is not as critical. An omnibus bill shows, in legal terms, what we need to achieve. It also shows that we are not seeking special rights because the main thing that we are doing is adding the terms *sexual orientation* and *gender identity* in places in current law that protect race, gender, national origin, and religion.

4. Identify the different paths that there are to achieve each goal: by the legislatures, by the courts, and by popular vote.

Different people and different organizations will take different paths to achieve each of the equality goals. Insofar we agree on the goals, different paths are fine because it is very difficult to know in advance which path will lead us to equality faster.

5. Endorse candidates for elected office with clear criteria. A good endorsement process needs to result in more than just an endorse-or-don't-endorse outcome. It is also important to make the endorsement criteria public.

6. Check that endorsed candidates, once elected, sponsor and vote for equality legislation.

7. Legislate to cover *all* the members of the LGBT community.

Understanding what needs to be done is not rocket science. The following chapters examine each of the steps, starting with each of the equality goals to be achieved.

22.

Equality Goal: Nondiscrimination

Mary gets to work to find a note from her boss to see him immediately. Upon entering his office, she can tell that something is wrong.

The boss tells her that she is being fired. She says, "You mean laid off?" The boss says, "No, you are being fired—no layoff package, no unemployment benefits."

Mary is in shock. She thinks about the twelve years she has spent with the company in Florida. In her mind, she goes through the annual raises, the promotions, the wonderful reviews.

She tells the boss, "Tell it to me straight. Why am I getting fired?" The boss doesn't want to tell. Finally, having known Mary for so many years, he talks. The boss says, "My new boss told me that he doesn't want dykes working here."

Mary calls a friend who is an attorney. The attorney says, "I don't need to think about the case very much." Mary is intrigued. The attorney friend continues, "There is absolutely nothing that anyone can do."

Mary is confused. In her state of Florida, like in the majority of states, if the company would have dismissed her by saying that her performance was not good enough, she could have fought it in court by asking them to prove it—given that her annual performance reviews clearly said the contrary. However, because she was dismissed for being a lesbian, there is nothing that she can do. Sexual orientation and gender identity and expression are not protected in her state nor in a majority of states. Nor is it protected with federal legislation.

Protection for sexual orientation also means protection if you are discriminated against for being heterosexual. Say that you are a bartender working in California in a gay bar and you get fired because you are heterosexual (this actually happened). Because

California has a nondiscrimination statute that covers sexual orientation and gender identity and expression, the heterosexual bartender got his job back because you do not need to be gay to be a good bartender in a gay bar.

One of the groups that suffer the most discrimination is people whose gender do not match their gender at birth. Transgender people get severely discriminated against in employment, housing, access to public assistance, and so many aspects vital to everyday life. So it is absolutely critical that, when seeking equality under the law, we always include sexual orientation *and* gender identity and expression.

Fortunately, on April 20, 2012, the EEOC (Equal Employment Opportunity Commission), in an unanimous ruling, decided that transgender and gender non-conforming individuals were covered under Title VII of the Civil Rights Act related to employment nondiscrimination. This ruling is notable, too, because the decision was unanimous, and commissioners were appointed by both Republican and Democratic presidents. So, after this important decision, the message to our transgender friends is: please do not leave your gay, lesbian, and bisexual friends behind!

Hopefully, the EEOC will be able to expand its ruling to cover all LGBT people by considering also that gays, lesbians, and bisexuals are intrinsically gender non-conforming.

The protections in the United States against discrimination are extensive, as one would expect in an advanced democracy. They include:

- Employment
- Housing
- Credit
- Public accommodation
- Public facilities
- Federally funded programs and activities

A comprehensive bill to protect against discrimination due to sexual orientation was introduced by Bella Abzug in 1974 in the House of Representatives. Year after year it was getting more cosponsors, but it never got voted on. Fifteen years later, in 1989, it was reintroduced, focusing only on employment and limited to sexual orientation under the strategy that a smaller legislation would have a higher chance to pass.

Despite this strategy of asking for less, forty years later there is still no federal law against discrimination in employment due to sexual orientation.

The current strategy is to include gender identity but be still limited to employment. Such legislation passed the Senate in 2013 by a margin of two to one, but it is not expected to be voted by the House any time soon.

Interestingly, most Americans believe that sexual orientation and gender identity and expression are already protected against discrimination in federal legislation and state laws. Here is the reality:

- There is no federal law protecting against discrimination based on sexual orientation or gender identity and expression.

- In twenty-nine states there is no protection against discrimination based on sexual orientation or gender identity or expression.

- In only sixteen states and the District of Columbia there is protection against discrimination based on sexual orientation and gender identity and expression.

- Five states provide limited protection.

As mentioned earlier, as of April 20, 2012, transgender and gender non-conforming individuals are the only LGBT people protected nationwide against employment discrimination thanks to an Equal Employment Opportunity Commission ruling.

There is still much work to be done to achieve the protection against discrimination in employment, housing, credit, public accommodation, public facilities, and federal funded programs that most Americans take for granted (and falsely believe is already available to lesbian, gay, bisexual, and transgender people).

Nondiscrimination is a critical battle for equality in our country because it affects so many people. Also, people cannot fight for other rights if they are concerned that they will be fired for being who they are. So the battle continues on this front, but we got a sliver of equality in one of the most revered institutions. Read on.

23.

Equality Goal: Marriage Equality

"Separate is never equal."

—The Dallas Principles,
Principle #3

The freedom to marry the person you love is the most prominent battle for equality in our country today. It has caught the imagination of a young generation, who cannot comprehend such discrimination. So, most people might expect this to be the longest chapter of the book.

It isn't.

That's because the argument couldn't be simpler: marriage equality represents the essence of who we are as a country. It represents freedom of religion. It demonstrates the key religious principle that it is not for me to judge others. It represents the pursuit of happiness. It represents the ideal that we live and let live. It represents that we encourage people taking care of each other in a lifelong commitment. It represents the idea that we do not want the government to dictate who we can marry. It is not about benefits and responsibilities; it is about showing your love and commitment to each other and the world with the word that everybody uses to express it: marriage. It is not about redefining marriage, it is expanding it by letting same-gender couples embrace the commitment that marriage means. It is about treating all couples equally. It is not about a separate, and unequal, institution such as civil unions, because separate is not equal.

It is very worthwhile to watch the documentary *Bridegroom*, which illustrates powerfully the love between two men in their twenties, Shane and Tom, and how they built their lives together, owning a business and a home, and adopting an adorable dog. Both share upbringings in small towns in Indiana and Montana with very different support from their families. They had moved to Los Angeles, where they met. In 2011, they committed to marry as soon as marriage was legal again in California (it was legal for part of 2008 and become finally legal in 2013). When Tom dies in a freak accident, the hospital refuses to allow Shane to see him. That this happened in a city like Los Angeles is unacceptable. What makes it worse is that this happened several months after new regulations came into effect in the whole country to avoid repetition of the Lisa Pond case in Miami (described in Chapter 3) in which a partner of eighteen years and their children were not allowed to be with Lisa as she was dying. *Bridegroom* goes to also describe the reaction of Tom's family. A love story interrupted by tragedy—very worth watching.

In their never ending pursuit to deny others the fundamental right to marry the person they love, people use five main arguments:

1. *"My religion says that marriage is between one man and one woman forever."*
   This is a very valid argument. You have all the right to believe so. Nobody can force your religion to marry same-gender couples or to allow divorces.

   At the same time, other religions believe that marriage is between two people who love each other—even if they are the same gender.

   So how do we ensure your freedom of religion and at the same time allow others their freedom of religion?

   It is quite simple: each religion can impose any constraints they want on whom to marry. We do not want the government to impose on you the wishes of another religion. So, the government issues *civil* marriage *licenses* according to its own criteria—one that treats all citizens the same regardless of their religion or their sexual orientation and gender identity and expression.

   This is the same argument for divorce: some religions allow divorce and some don't. Still the government allows divorce. In fact, the first no fault divorce law in the country was signed in 1969 by Ronald Reagan, then the governor of California.

2. *"What about the sanctity of marriage?"*

Most religions consider marriage to be sacred. Naturally, only those couples who have married in that Church according to the Church teachings are bound by that sacred relationship. People married in a civil marriage, however, chose to be bound by civil laws and not by religious law in their marriage. Civil marriage and religious marriage are totally different.

3. *"For three thousand years, marriage has been between one man and one woman."*

This argument shows a complete ignorance of our history: several Native American tribes were polygamous; furthermore, the Mormon Church supported "plural marriages" (one man, several women) until 1890.

4. *"Why not confer the same obligations and benefits of marriage except for the word 'marriage'? Why not just have civil unions?"*

This was the position of President Obama until he concluded his personal evolution on May 9, 2012. Civil unions are a different institution, which is separate and discriminatory. It is a separate statute from marriage, and we have learned in our country that separate is not equal. In addition, it is discriminatory because it only applies to LGBT people.

5. *"Isn't marriage an issue for the states?"*

Marriage is indeed based on state law, but it is also a federal issue.

In June 2013, the US Supreme Court repealed the part of the Defense of Marriage Act, that prohibited the federal government from recognizing otherwise legal marriages of same-gender couples.

However, we still need to ensure that legal marriages are recognized anywhere in the country. Imagine that you are a heterosexual couple and that your marriage is not recognized in certain states. What would happen to your freedom to travel and relocate? Beyond that, if marriage is such a fundamental right, then all states should confer it to all loving couples, as the US Supreme Court will do in a very few years.

A well-respected Republican pollster, Jan van Lohuizen, found out that until 2009, support for marriage equality was increasing at a rate of 1 percent per year. Since then, it has been increasing at 5 percent per year across all age groups and party affiliations. In 2013, more than half of Americans polled supported marriage equality.

Many organizations are involved in achieving marriage equality, but Freedom To Marry (FreedomToMarry.org) focuses exclusively on achieving this equality goal.

We can have freedom of religion while letting all loving and committed couples take care of each other. Let's then discuss other equality goals.

24.

Equality Goal: Protecting Youth

One of our obligations in society is to protect our youth, especially in schools, in places of worship, and in homes.

We have to do much better.

What are the effects on LGBT youth when they become homeless because their parents throw them out of the house, while still underage, for being gay? What happens when schools are not allowed to teach about sexual orientation or cannot teach about protection to avoid pregnancy and sexually transmitted diseases? What happens when children, and especially LGBT children, are mistreated in the foster care system? What happens when LGBT youth hear the repeated anti-equality messages from so many elected officials? From their teachers? From their parents? What happens when heterosexual children are mistreated just because their parents are LGBT?

Are we a society who cares about our youth or not? Do we provide the safe space in which they can develop to their full potential? Studies show that 85 percent of LGBT students in middle and high school suffered from harassment in the prior school year (check www.GLSEN.org for their pioneering research). Harassment does not lend itself to a safe environment for youth to study, grow, and develop.

Too many young people have suffered due to some wrong-headed beliefs and actions from some elected public officials, some parents, some educators, some priests and church leaders, and other people who are supposed to help our youth. In 2010, all of this came to a head. In July that year, Justin Aaberg, a gay fifteen-year old, died by suicide in Minnesota. In September, it was Tyler Clementi, eighteen, a gay freshman at Rutgers University. Billy Lucas, fifteen and gay, from Indiana, also died by suicide. There was a national outrage, which resulted in a White House summit on bullying. An important resource to recommend to youth in distress is www.TheTrevorProject.org, which provides crisis intervention and suicide prevention services for LGBT youth.

More than twenty-five years ago, Harvey Milk, the openly gay member of the San Francisco Board of Supervisors who was killed in 1978 by another member of that board, put it best:

> And the young gay people in the Altoona, Pennsylvanias, and the Richmond, Minnesotas, who are coming out and hear Anita Bryant in television and her story. The only thing they have to look forward to is hope. And you have to give them hope. Hope for a better world, hope for a better tomorrow, hope for a better place to come to if the pressures at home are too great. Hope that all will be all right. Without hope, not only gays, but the blacks, the seniors, the handicapped, the us'es, the us'es will give up.

We have not solved the problem yet. LGBT youth continue to suffer tremendously. In September 2010, Dan Savage, a gay columnist, followed a few days later by Joel Burns, a city council member in Fort Worth, Texas, sent a message of hope to teenagers by stating that "It Gets Better." The video by Joel has been watched more than 2.8 million times, and the video from Dan and his husband, Terry, almost 1.9 million times.

As part of the www.ItGetsBetter.org project, many videos have been created and posted online. Here is a startling comparison about political leaders who made an It Gets Better video and whether their counterparts did or not:

- The president of the United States, Barack Obama, found the time to make a video for ItGetsBetter.org.

- The vice president of the United States, Joe Biden, did one, too.

- Republican presidential contenders Mitt Romney and Paul Ryan did not.

- Former Democratic speaker Nancy Pelosi also made a video.

- Republican speaker John Boehner did not.

The list could go on and on. If we cannot take care of all of our children, what type of society are we?

Protecting our youth also means protecting the straight children of LGBT parents. COLAGE.org is an organization for young people with lesbian, gay, bisexual, or transgender parents.

The message to our youth is that *it gets better*. It is true that, after the teenage years, things change and do get better but not because the laws are equal. You can still be fired. You still cannot marry in most states. And so on. It does get better because you can associate with people who respect you instead of immature middle and high school bullies. Still, however, you will face adult bullies who do not respect the principle that we were all created equal and should be treated equally under the law.

The responsibility of the adults is to *make it better* for bullied youth. We need to pass anti-bullying legislation to end the torment of so many of our young people. We also need to show that we have created a society in which everybody is truly treated the same under the law.

The need for acting against bullying is pressing as it takes a new scale with bullying through the internet ("cyber bullying"), which impacts large number of teenagers—gay and non-gay.

It is time now to address the next equality goal, also related to children.

25.

Equality Goal: Same-Gender Parenting

"In America, no two families look the same."

—President Barack Obama,
November 1, 2012

Many same-gender couples, like other couples, want to form their own families and have children. This is a fundamental human feeling and a basic right that brings stability to society. For the protection of children, it is very important to have legislation that treats all families equally under the law.

In October 2012, Sophia Bailey-Klugh, a ten-year-old, sent a letter to President Obama. It was unprompted by her parents. Here is the letter:

Dear Barack Obama,

It's Sophia Bailey Klugh your friend who invited you to dinner. You don't remember okay that's fine. But I just wanted to tell you that I am so glad you agree that two men can love each other because I have two dads and they love each other. But at school kids think that it's gross and weird but it really hurts my heart and feelings. So I come to you because you are my hero. If you were me and had two dads that love each other, and kids at school teased you about it, what would you do?

Please respond!

I just wanted to say you really inspire me. I hope you win on being the president. You would totally make the world better place.

Your friend Sophia.

P.S. Please tell your daughters Hi for me!

On November 1, in the mist of his reelection campaign, the president responded:

Thank you for writing me such a thoughtful letter about your family. Reading it made me proud to be your president and even more hopeful about the future of our nation.

In America, no two families look the same. We celebrate this diversity. And we recognize that whether you have two dads or one mom what matters above all is the love we show one another. You are very fortunate to have two parents who care deeply for you. They are lucky to have such an exceptional daughter in you.

Our differences unite us. You and I are blessed to live in a country where we are born equal no matter what we look like in the outside, where we grow up, or who our parents are. A good rule is to treat others the way you hope they will treat you. Remind your friends at school about this rule if they say something that hurts your feelings.

Thanks again for taking the time to write me. I'm honored to have your support and inspired by your compassion. I'm sorry I couldn't make it to dinner, but I'll be sure to tell Sasha and Malia you say hello.

Sincerely,

Barack Obama

President Obama described the reality of what America is about and our desire to be a diverse, vibrant culture. The question is: can same-gender parents be as effective as different-gender parents? Scientific research clearly shows that the answer is yes.

Here is what the American Academy of Pediatrics has to say about it: (healthychildren.org/English/family-life/family-dynamics/types-of-families/pages/Gay-and-Lesbian-Parents.aspx)

> Studies have shown that children with gay and/or lesbian parents are ultimately just as happy with themselves and their own gender as are their friends with heterosexual parents. Children whose parents are homosexual show no difference in their choice of friends, activities, or interests compared to children whose parents are heterosexual. As adults, their career choices and lifestyles are similar to those of children raised by heterosexual parents.
>
> Research comparing children raised by homosexual parents to children raised by heterosexual parents has found no developmental differences in intelligence, psychological adjustment, social adjustment, or peer popularity between them. Children raised by homosexual parents can and do have fulfilling relationships with their friends as well as romantic relationships later on.

Here is the conclusion from a report of the American Academy of Pediatrics: (neoreviews.aappublications.org/content/pediatrics/118/1/349.full)

> There is ample evidence to show that children raised by same-gender parents fare as well as those raised by heterosexual parents. More than 25 years of research have documented that there is no relationship between parents' sexual orientation and any measure of a child's emotional, psychosocial, and behavioral adjustment. These data have demonstrated no risk to children as a result of growing up in a family with 1 or more gay parents. Conscientious and nurturing adults, whether they are men or women, heterosexual or homosexual, can be excellent parents. The rights,

benefits, and protections of civil marriage can further strengthen these families.

Below, in very clear terms, is the conclusion from the American Psychological Association:
(www.apa.org/helpcenter/sexual-orientation.aspx)

> Social science has shown that the concerns often raised about children of lesbian and gay parents— concerns that are generally grounded in prejudice against and stereotypes about gay people—are unfounded. Overall, the research indicates that the children of lesbian and gay parents do not differ markedly from the children of heterosexual parents in their development, adjustment, or overall well-being.

Professor Judith Stacey of New York University summarizes it very well:
(en.wikipedia.org/wiki/LGBT_parenting)

> Rarely is there as much consensus in any area of social science as in the case of gay parenting, which is why the American Academy of Pediatrics and all of the major professional organizations with expertise in child welfare have issued reports and resolutions in support of gay and lesbian parental rights.

The scientific evidence is clear. Despite this, in 2008, the state of Florida spent $120,000 of taxpayers' money for the testimony of Dr. George Alan Rekers, who was paid to testify in opposition to a lawsuit asking to allow single LGBT people to adopt in Florida— like they can do in *all* other states. Dr. Rekers, a professor and ordained Southern Baptist minister, has written extensively about homosexuality, parenting, and conversion therapy. He also testified on multiple occasions in the past against parenthood by LGBT people, as well as testifying that homosexuality is sinful.

Dr. Rekers has been a major player in denying LGBT people their equality. In the ultimate irony and hypocrisy, it was discovered that in May 2010 Dr. Rekers hired a male prostitute from www.RentBoy.com for a ten-day trip to London and Madrid, with detailed duties for his escort. These duties included sexual massages. Frank Rich wrote in the *New York Times* on May 15, 2010:

> Thanks to Rekers's clownish public exposure, we now know that his professional judgments are windows into *his* cracked psyche, not gay people's. But there is nothing funny about the destruction his writings and public activities have sown. His fringe views have not remained on the fringe. His excursions into public policy have had real and damaging consequences on a large swath of Americans.

The suitability of an individual or a couple to be adoptive parents is always reviewed on a case-by-case basis. However, some states discriminate if the individual or couple is lesbian, gay, bisexual, or transgender, without giving them the opportunity to demonstrate that they can be good parents.

We need equal treatment under the law in the three types of adoption:

1. *Adoption by an individual who is single*

   Until 2010, Florida was the only state in which there was an explicit prohibition for LGBT people to adopt, whether single or in a relationship. An ACLU lawsuit resulted in a ruling on September 22, 2010, that such a ban was unconstitutional. On October 12, 2010, the Florida Department of Children and Families decided not to appeal the case. Finally, single LGBT people can now legally adopt in each state of the Union.

2. *Adoption by a same-gender couple*

   In ten states (California, Connecticut, District of Columbia, Illinois, Indiana, Maine, Massachusetts, New Jersey, New York, Oregon, and Vermont) and the District of Columbia, there is specific legislation allowing LGBT couples to adopt. In addition, in two states (Nevada and New Hampshire), same-sex couples have been able to adopt in some jurisdictions. On the other side of the spectrum, Mississippi expressly forbids same-gender couples to adopt. Utah does not allow unmarried couples to adopt; since Utah does not recognize same-sex marriages from other states, same-gender couples cannot adopt there.

3. *Adoption by a member of a same-gender couple of the other's child (called second-parent adoption)*

Four states authorize second-parent adoption for same-gender couples in their statutes (California, Colorado, Connecticut, and Vermont). In six states and the District of Columbia, appellate courts have ruled that second-parent adoption is allowed for same-sex couples (Illinois, Indiana, Massachusetts, New York, New Jersey, Pennsylvania and the District of Columbia). In one state, Utah, legislation expressly prohibits second-parent adoption. In three states, appellate courts have determined that second-parent adoption is not allowed for same-sex couples (Nebraska, Ohio, and Wisconsin). In the rest of the states, the law is not clear, and in some cases trial courts have allowed second-parent adoption. In Oklahoma, a ban on recognition of same-sex adoptions from other states was challenged and won in court in 2006 by Lambda Legal.

There is much work to be done in the states to achieve full equality in adoption by same-gender couples. All the major LGBT legal organizations have been involved and have been very successful with adoption cases. These organizations are:

- ACLU Lesbian and Gay Rights Project (ACLU.org/LGBT-rights)

- Gay and Lesbian Defenders & Advocates (GLAD.org)

- Lambda Legal (LambdaLegal.org)

- National Center for Lesbian Rights (NCLRights.org)

Along with the work in the states, we need to pass federal legislation—in particular, the Every Child Deserves a Family Act, which does not allow discrimination based on sexual orientation, gender identity, or marital status of the prospective adoptive or foster parent or the sexual orientation or gender identity of the child involved. The standard, in every situation, should be based on the best interests of the child.

Given the scientific evidence and the absolute need for more adoptive and foster parents, it is horrible that some people want to deny children a loving home. Our country is better than that.

A related issue for a parent who is LGBT is to be able to keep custody of his or her child. Custody is customarily decided by the courts in the best interest of the child. One of the most famous cases is the one of Mary Ward, a lesbian who lost custody of her daughter in Florida in 1995 when the judge stated that the daughter should go live with her father, John Ward, to "live in a non-lesbian world."

It did not matter that, by all accounts, the mother was taking great care of the daughter while the father did not express much interest in custody... and the father had been convicted of killing his prior wife. It gets better: he killed her on a rage about custody of their daughter. And then, she sexually abused that daughter. Despite all of this, the judge decide to give custody to him. The documentary about the case is worth watching, *Unfit: Ward vs. Ward*.

Let's discuss the next equality goal.

26.

Equality Goal: Freedom of Gender

"Transgender discrimination is the civil rights issue
of our time."

—Vice President Joe Biden,
October 30, 2012

The majority of people understand the reality that sexual orientation is clearly part of a spectrum ranging from heterosexuality to homosexuality, with a middle ground of bisexuality.

However, most people see gender identity as binary: you are either male or female. The reality is that this is not what happens in nature. While the vast majority of us are either male or female, the Intersex Society of North America defines intersex as "a variety of conditions in which a person is born with a reproductive or sexual anatomy that doesn't seem to fit the typical definitions of female or male" and estimates that "the total of people whose bodies differ from standard male or female is one in 100 births." This is a complex medical issue that goes well beyond having a Y chromosome or not.

You may not have heard of the term "intersex" before and therefore wonder whether this is a new condition. Actually, it has been documented for at least eighteen hundred years. A great example can be found in the Louvre Museum: a sculpture of a beautiful naked female body lying on a marble mattress but with male genitalia. The sculpture is called the "Hermaphrodite Endormi" ("Sleeping Hermaphrodite").

So not everybody is clearly male or female from a physical perspective. Similarly, there are people who know that their true gender is not the gender of their birth. As an advanced society, with knowledge based on scientific analysis, we understand the need people have to live their true gender.

Transgender and intersex are different conditions, and organizations fighting for the rights of transgender people and intersex people try to keep them as separate issues. We respect this but note that both intersex and transgender people suffer tremendous discrimination and prejudices from people who are not familiar with the facts.

Similarly, some people are uncomfortable when people do not behave in the expected roles of male or female (this is called gender expression)—maybe a female who is "too butch" or a male who is "too effeminate" or a cross-dresser or a person dressed in a gender-ambivalent manner. Note that gender expression is different from sexual orientation. In any of the examples above, the person might be heterosexual, homosexual, or bisexual.

Many people feel more comfortable with a binary world ("black or white"), but this is not the real world or the world of nature.

Here are some of the hurdles and discriminatory treatment that people face about their gender identity or expression:

- Employment discrimination (fortunately since 2102, there are legal recourses)

- Lack of healthcare access and insurance coverage

- Inability to declare the appropriate gender in documents (passport, driver's license, Social Security database, and voting ID) to avoid confusion in real life. Several of these issues have been resolved by the Obama administration.

- Access to restrooms

- Air travel scrutiny

- Gender stereotyping

- Military medical and uniform regulations that discriminate against transgender service members

Some people have misgivings about allowing the freedom of gender. Some of these misgivings may be rooted in religious beliefs. Certainly people have the right to hold those beliefs. Other people have the religious belief that God created a complex natural environment, which includes a variety of sexual orientations, gender identities and expressions.

There is a new generation of people who see gender identity and expression as a spectrum, not necessarily male or female. Like bisexual for sexual orientation, some people identify their sexual identity as bi-gender. This fluidity may be difficult to understand for the majority of people, who were born being comfortable with their biological gender.

A good representative of the new thinking is Stephen Ira. He is the twenty-two-year-old son of actor Warren Beatty and actress Annette Bening. He was born female and transitioned to male at age fourteen and concluded at age seventeen that he was gay. Stephen's video *WeHappyTrans* has received more than half a million views on YouTube. In this video, you can clearly see the looks and facial expressions of his father.

There are some notable organizations working on this goal of freedom of gender: the National Center for Transgender Equality (TransEquality.org), the TransgenderLawCenter.org, and the Woodhull Sexual Freedom Alliance (WoodhullAlliance.org), which takes the perspective of sexual freedom as a fundamental human right.

Most Americans share a common respect for our Constitution and the belief of not letting the government interfere in our most intimate decisions. Because of that, we need to ensure that people with a different gender identity or expression are treated equally under the law and can pursue their personal happiness free from discrimination.

Let's look into the next equality goal in the following chapter—a goal partially achieved.

27.

Equality Goal: Serving in the Military

Finally, on September 20, 2011, the repeal of "Don't Ask, Don't Tell" took effect. This was the legislation passed in 1993 that forced many service members, who are risking their lives for our freedom, to have to live a lie and not have the freedom to be themselves. The support for repeal had become just too big to ignore: 77 percent of Americans supporting repeal (*Washington Post/ABC News* poll, December 15, 2010).

The legislation to repeal "Don't Ask, Don't Tell" was passed in December 2010:

- The House of Representatives voted 250 to 175 for the repeal. Of those voting in favor, 94 percent were Democrats and 6 percent were Republicans. Of those voting against the repeal, 91 percent were Republicans and 9 percent Democrats.

- The Senate voted 65 to 33 for repeal. Of those voting in favor, 88 percent were Democrats or Independents, and 12 percent were Republicans. Of those voting against the repeal, 100 percent were Republican.

However, to gain some Republican support, the legislation was modified at the last moment to eliminate the clause that stated that service members cannot be discriminated against because of their sexual orientation. Under the new law, service members can disclose their sexual orientation without being discharged, however, they can still be discriminated in promotions and other matters.

It took more than seventeen years to repeal "Don't Ask, Don't Tell." It was a momentous achievement. However, we were let down by a Congress that did only half the job. How many more years until we add sexual orientation to the nondiscrimination policies of the military? How many more years until we allow transgender members to serve?

Many organizations helped in the repeal of "Don't Ask, Don't Tell," but two of them played a key, long-term role: Servicemembers Legal Defense Network (SLDN.org), which merged with OutServe in 2012, and Palm Center (PalmCenter.org). These organizations are evolving their missions for the new set of needs.

In addition, several individuals led by Lt. Dan Choi and assisted by a new organization, GetEqual.org, added tremendous visibility to the fight not only with the public but also with elected officials, including President Obama and Senate Majority Leader Reid.

It is time to discuss the last equality goal—one that has been achieved at the federal level, but not in most states.

28.

Equality Goal: Hate-Crimes Legislation

This equality goal was achieved at the federal level on October 28, 2009, when President Obama signed into law the Matthew Shepard and James Byrd, Jr. Hate Crimes Prevention Act.

This federal law was named after two well-publicized hate-crime victims who suffered horrifying deaths. James Byrd, Jr., was a heterosexual African-American who was dragged from a pickup truck by three white supremacists in Texas. He was conscious through most of the ordeal, until his head and arm were severed when hitting a curb. The three supremacists continued to drive the truck, dragging the headless body for more than a mile. At that time, in 1998, Texas did not have a hate-crime statute (now it has one, but it does not cover gender identity or expression). The second person for whom the bill is named is Matthew Shepard, a gay student who, also in 1998, was beaten and left to die on a fence in Laramie, Wyoming. At the time, Wyoming did not have any hate-crime statutes either and still does not have one.

Although equality and protection of people would be expected to be a nonpartisan issue, the Matthew Shepard and James Byrd, Jr. Hate Crimes Prevention Act passed Congress in a very partisan manner, like the repeal of "Don't Ask, Don't Tell":

- In the House of Representatives, the vote was 249 in favor to 175 opposed. Of the votes in favor, 93 percent were cast by Democrats. Of the votes against the legislation, 90 percent were from Republicans.

- In the Senate, the vote was sixty-three to twenty-eight (with nine senators not voting). Of the sixty-three senators voting in favor, 92 percent were Democrats or Independents (Senators Lieberman and Sanders), while all the twenty-eight senators voting against it were Republicans.

The statistics above may appear partisan. The reality is that equality is still a partisan matter in the United States: the majority of Democratic legislators vote in favor of equality while the majority of Republican legislators vote against it.

Equality should not be a partisan matter. Legislators of any party affiliation should agree to what most of the population already agrees with: every person should be treated equally under the law. A Hart Research poll in 2007 (two years before the legislation was approved) showed that 73 percent of Americans supported hate-crime legislation covering sexual orientation and gender identity and expression. More interestingly:

- Fifty-six percent of Republican men supported hate-crime legislation.

- Sixty-three percent of Evangelical Christians supported it, too.

The definition of sexual orientation covers not only homosexuality, but heterosexuality and bisexuality. So, it is a protection for every person (although note that some people identify as asexual).

While this equality goal has been achieved at the federal level, still much work remains to be done in the states.

There are many misunderstandings about hate-crime legislation:

CLAIM: If a crime is already penalized, there's no need to penalize more because the motivation was hate.

REALITY: Penalties imposed by the judicial system are usually based on motivation and intent. If someone kills somebody by accident, the penalty is less severe than if there was premeditation. Likewise, the penalty should be different when the motivation was hate.

CLAIM: Sexual orientation concerns a special group, and, therefore, sexual orientation does not need to be protected under the law.

REALITY: The law already protects other special groups subject to attack (for example, due to religious beliefs). The law needs to protect sexual-orientation and gender-identity victims because about the same number of them are attacked per year as are those attacked due to their religious beliefs. In addition, sexual orientation covers, by definition, heterosexuals, homosexuals, and bisexuals.

CLAIM: Sexual orientation is a choice (it is not innate), therefore it should not be protected.

REALITY: Science demonstrates that sexual orientation is innate. However, even if it were a choice, it should be protected since religious beliefs (which are clearly a choice) are protected.

CLAIM: Pastors may be tried under this legislation if, after their giving a sermon, a member of the congregation commits a hate crime motivated by the sermon.

REALITY: The hate-crime legislation explicitly includes First Amendment protections toward speech. Hate-crime legislation is about actions and bodily harm against somebody. Freedom of speech is always protected: we are always free to think and talk, even hateful speech. Supporters of this legislation included the Presbyterian and Episcopal Churches.

CLAIM: Federal hate-crime legislation means that the federal government will be interfering with local police.

REALITY: The hate-crime legislation has been endorsed by virtually all major law enforcement organizations (including the International Association of Chiefs of Police, the National District Attorneys Association, the National Sheriffs Association, the Police Executive Research Forum, etc.). The police force understands the hideousness of these crimes.

Why is investigating and penalizing hate crimes so important?

The FBI has a clear answer on its website:

> Investigating hate crime is the number one priority of our Civil Rights Program. Why? Not only because hate crime has a devastating impact on families and communities, but also because groups that preach hatred and intolerance plant the seeds of terrorism here in our country.

The most recent FBI statistics indicate that in 2012 there were 1,318 victims of hate crimes in the United States due to sexual orientation. This is about the same number of victims (1,166) due to religion. It is very important to cover in legislation both types of hate crimes.

Since 1968, there has been a federal hate-crime law that penalizes violent crimes against individuals due to their race, religion, and ethnic origin. It is well understood that there should be an additional penalty when somebody hurts somebody intentionally motivated by hate toward the victim's religion, race, or origin.

However, for forty-one years, there was no federal hate-crime legislation covering such obvious targets as gender and disability until Congress passed this important legislation in 2009.

Let's examine now how we keep score of the progress on all of these equality goals.

29.

Keeping Score

"Success is measured by the civil rights we all achieve, not by words, access or money raised."

—The Dallas Principles,
Principle #7

It is critical to keep track of progress toward legal equality. To that effect, eQualityGiving (which I cofounded) pioneered two measurements: one at the federal level and one at the state level.

At the federal level, there are thirteen major areas of federal law in which LGBT people are not treated equally. These areas are addressed by the seven equality goals; some of these goals are counted separately since they may be considered by separate committees in Congress. Under this measurement, we have achieved:

- Hate-crime legislation passed at the federal level—full goal achieved

- Repeal of "Don't Ask, Don't Tell" has been achieved, but there is no protection against discrimination—so, partial goal achieved

- Nondiscrimination in employment has been achieved only for transgender and gender non-conforming persons— partial goal achieved

- Marriage equality at the federal level has been fully achieved but only for couples while they are in a nondiscriminatory state. So, goal is partially achieved.

- Immigration equality has been achieved thanks to the Supreme Court ruling of June 26, 2013.

So the rating is now 3.5 out of thirteen (counting partial goals as half a point) or 27 percent; this is up from 15 percent in 2013 thanks to the Supreme Court rulings, but we still have a long way to go to be 100 percent equal under federal law. The reality is that this is not rocket science. We know what needs to be done; it is all written in an omnibus bill prepared by attorney Karen Doering at the request of eQualityGiving (see next chapter).

Much more progress has been made at the state level—although only in a handful of states. For each state, we keep track of six of the seven equality goals (we do not track the goal to serve in the military since most states follow federal law for their national guard). Four states and the District of Columbia have reached a score of 100 percent legal equality for their LGBT residents. Can you guess which states they are?

If you thought Massachusetts, this was a good logical choice since it was the first state to offer marriage equality. However, it only scores 83 percent since it is missing a couple of important protections for transgender people.

The four states that have 100 percent equality for LGBT individuals are California, Connecticut, New Jersey, and Vermont. Several states are very close: Colorado, Illinois, Iowa, Massachusetts, Minnesota, New York, and Washington.

Here is an example of why it is important to keep score with uniform measurements: one large state LGBT organization prepared its own study of progress in its state and concluded that the state was in the top five states for protecting LGBT individuals from discrimination. The reality is different: the eQualityGiving measure rates their state at 25 percent (which places it toward the bottom). One example of the discrepancy in the results is that the state organization gives itself credit for having a statewide statute protecting against bullying. That statute, however, does not list specific categories of protected youth. Research by GLSEN shows that without enumeration such legislation is not effective at all on protecting individuals.

Do you know where your state stands in LGBT equality?

Take the following quiz:

1. HATE CRIMES: Does your state have hate-crime laws that address violent crimes against individuals due to their sexual orientation *and* gender identity and expression?

   a) Yes
   b) Only sexual orientation is covered in state law
   c) No state law (only federal law)
   d) Don't know

2. NONDISCRIMINATION: Does your state have laws that forbid discrimination in employment for both private and public employers as well as in housing, finance, and public accommodations due to sexual orientation *and* gender identity and expression?

   a) Yes
   b) Mostly: sexual orientation and gender identity covered with the exception of public accommodation protection for gender identity
   c) Only sexual orientation covered
   d) No state law
   e) Don't know

3. CIVIL MARRIAGE EQUALITY: Does your state have laws allowing same-gender couples to marry (i.e., get the same civil marriage license as different-gender couples)?

   a) Yes
   b) Civil unions only
   c) Domestic partnerships only
   d) No
   e) Don't know

4. FREEDOM OF GENDER: Does your state allow a transgender person to obtain a new birth certificate indicating the correct gender?

   a) Yes
   b) Amended certificate (which shows the prior gender)
   c) Decided by court order
   d) Depends on city clerk
   e) No
   f) Don't know

5. PROTECTING YOUTH: Does your state have anti-bullying/anti-harassment laws that specifically list sexual orientation *and* gender identity and expression?

a) Yes
b) Only sexual orientation listed
c) No
d) Don't know

6. SAME-GENDER PARENTING RIGHTS: Does your state allow all qualified LGBT individuals and same-gender couples to jointly adopt, as well as allowing second-parent adoption?

a) Yes
b) Only single LGBT people can adopt
c) Only single or joint adoption, but not second-parent adoption
d) It depends on the jurisdiction—some do allow it
e) Not tested—full extent of parental rights not known
f) No
g) Don't know

You can check the answers for any state and the District of Columbia here: www.eQualityGiving.org/States-of-Equality-and-Gay-Rights-Scorecard.

As the federal and state measurements show, more progress has been made on LGBT legal equality in the states than in the federal government. In four states (California, Connecticut, New Jersey, and Vermont) and the District of Columbia, the answer to all the questions above is *yes*. However, in the other forty-six states, LGBT people are not treated equally under the law.

Why are we shortchanging our beloved Constitution and not providing the equal protection under the law that it promises? The next chapter tackles this question.

30.

Equal Once and for All

"Equal laws protecting equal rights... the best
guarantee of loyalty and love of country."

—James Madison

In 2005, eQualityGiving created the equality goals. As we have
seen, this is the simple expression in plain English of what is
needed for LGBT people to be equal under the law. Interestingly
enough, the majority (if not all) of the LGBT organizations
structure their websites in terms of *issues* instead of *goals*. This
has an impact on focus, approach, measurements, and what
constitutes success. It has an impact on endorsements for elected
office as well as the expectations about what these candidates
should do once they are elected.

In late 2008, eQualityGiving engaged Karen Doering, a well-
respected attorney and expert on nondiscrimination legislation, to
review federal legislation and prepare a model omnibus legislation
to bring equality under the law to LGBT people. The result of her
work was the Equality and Religious Freedom Act. It covers
thirteen areas of federal law in which we are not yet treated
equally:

1. Employment in the private sector
2. Employment in the federal government
3. Housing
4. Public accommodation
5. Public facilities
6. Credit
7. Federally funded programs and activities
8. Education
9. Disability
10. Civil marriage
11. Hate crimes (signed into law on October 28, 2009)

12. Armed forces (The "Don't Ask, Don't Tell" Repeal Act was signed into law on December 22, 2010)
13. Immigration

You can download the proposed bill here:
www.eQualityGiving.org/Blueprint-for-LGBT-Equality

Some people say it is not a good idea to introduce an omnibus bill in Congress since it would have to be divided into pieces and be submitted to and get approval from different subcommittees. This is true, but here are the important reasons to introduce an omnibus bill:

1. *Putting it in writing*

   Since we are seeking legal equality, it is obvious that we need to have a proposed bill with all our goals. This constitutes the gold standard of what is missing to be equal under the law.

2. *No more than others*

   The proposed bill demonstrates that LGBT people do not seek "special rights" as the bill basically adds the terms *sexual orientation* and *gender identity* to existing legislation.

3. *No less than others*

   This bill is also the standard to compare to partial legislation if approved in smaller pieces. How does a bill compare to the appropriate section of the omnibus bill? Are there any last-minute amendments that compromise our equality? This actually happened in the final negotiations to repeal "Don't Ask, Don't Tell"—important protections were cut at the last moment, as discussed in Chapter 27.

Once you understand the purpose of an omnibus bill, you will understand that cutting parts of it in the name of compromise means that *rights get denied.*

A month after eQualityGiving presented the omnibus bill in April 2009, a freshman member of the House of Representatives, Jared

Polis (who is gay), said that he would be interested in sponsoring such a bill. Two years later, in 2011, he was seeking comments about what to include. As of November 2013, his proposed bill, which is just a compilation of existing bills, has not been introduced. In the meantime, more than 135 LGBT organizations have signed a request for such legislation.

Some legislative efforts are difficult. For instance, creating a healthcare overhaul requires significant knowledge of how the industry operates, its effects on patients, and the various approaches to solving the problem. However, equal rights legislation is not difficult to conceive. What to include? Simply include everything in which LGBT people do not have the same rights as others. This is why it is called omnibus legislation. It should be the gold standard—not just a compilation of bills with their own compromises.

How do we raise awareness of the urgency for equality? Read on.

31.

What Happened in Dallas?

Two dozen activists, donors, strategists, and former executive directors got together in Dallas on the weekend of May 15–17, 2009, and drafted a unique document called "The Dallas Principles."

The essence of the Dallas Principles is simple:

Full LGBT Equality Now. No Delays. No Excuses.

This may appear like an obvious declaration. It was as obvious then as it is now, and it was as relevant then as it is today. However, in the last four years, we have heard plenty of excuses to delay equality.

Here is the background: just after President Obama was first elected in November 2008, as well as during the transition and early months of his presidency, there was interaction between his team and several LGBT organizations. The expectations were high. Everybody understood that there were important priorities to address first (the economy was in shambles, and his policy priority was healthcare). However, it was clear to some of us that many in the LGBT movement were too willing to wait for "the proper time" to achieve equality and that they were buying into the administration's approach to do it incrementally over many years.

eQualityGiving wanted to motivate everybody to push for equality right then, when the conditions were more favorable than they had been in decades, with pro-equality Democrats controlling the White House, the House, and the Senate.

In this spirit, we contacted several people to join us in Dallas. We were careful to select people who were not currently heads of organizations and were mindful of having a balanced representation of gender, sexual orientation, gender identity, and race, as well as different skills and backgrounds. They all accepted, but some had to cancel at the last moment.

Why Dallas? Because it allowed the participants, who came from all over the country, to meet midway (nobody except for the moderator was from Dallas). This would ensure that people wouldn't join just because it was convenient. They really needed to have the commitment to come. Why a couple of dozen people? We wanted to ensure that the meeting was manageable and would create an end product. Everyone had to have a chance to be heard and participate fully.

So, while eQualityGiving convened the Dallas meeting, the Dallas Principles were created as a joint effort of the two dozen authors, everybody participating and everybody sweating the details to have a great product.

What was the impact of the Dallas Principles?

First, it has become very clear that we were right to push for equality immediately. To the dismay of many LGBT organizations, equality did not flow at the speed that they expected in late 2008 and early 2009. We were making progress but not in the timeframe, in the quantity, or at the quality that was expected. Then, in 2010, the Democrats lost control of the House as well as many seats in the Senate, and progress come to a standstill (as the Dallas Principles group had predicted).

Second, the Human Rights Campaign started a campaign (which included selling T-shirts) with the slogan "No Excuses" which is part of the Dallas Principles slogan of "Full Equality Now. No Delays. No Excuses."

Third, the Dallas Principles became known well beyond the LGBT community. Vice President Biden was made aware of them, as were key White House staffers, key members of Congress, and members of the Democratic National Committee.

Fourth, the Florida LGBT Democratic Caucus adopted the Dallas Principles as its platform for 2012. After that, for the first time in US history, the platform of a major political party (the Democratic Party) treated LGBT people as fully equal citizens, including the freedom to marry. The Republican Party platform of 2012 is similar to the 2008 platform: an insult to LGBT Americans. Note that the Green Party adopted many years ago a fully pro-LGBT-equality platform.

Fifth, another positive impact of the Dallas Principles is that there is a growing conversation about *full equality NOW*. However, many still say, "I support full LGBT equality now—*but* now is not the time because we do not have a majority in the House," or any other reason. So, in reality, these people do not believe in full equality now; they believe in *equality later*.

As Dr. Martin Luther King, Jr., said: "A right delayed is a right denied." How quickly we forget.

So, take your sides: are you for *equality now* or *equality later*?

If you are for equality now, you can sign up as an endorser of the Dallas Principles at www.ActOnPrinciples.org/endorsers.

The text of the Dallas Principles and information on its authors is listed in Appendix 2.

Let's examine next what is needed to have an inclusive movement for equality.

32.

A Movement for All

"We will not leave any part of our community
behind."

—The Dallas Principles,
Principle #2

For a movement that asks for legal equality for everybody, it is important that we show diversity in all of our efforts. All heads of LGBT organizations believe in diversity. However, much more needs to be done to really show that it is a diverse movement.

SEXUAL ORIENTATION DIVERSITY

Too many people are still mistrusting those who self-identify as bisexuals. They think that bisexuals are closeted gays or lesbians. Granted, bisexuals are a minority of the population, and, granted, when they are acting on their opposite gender attraction, they do not suffer the same discrimination as homosexual individuals. Bisexuals are still misunderstood and not represented appropriately in the LGBT movement (including boards of directors).

For the first time in American history, an openly bisexual person has been elected to Congress. In November 2012, Kyrsten Sinema was elected from Arizona.

Furthermore, beyond understanding bisexual people, there are many differences that need to be addressed between gays and lesbians in their approach to giving, politics, and social needs. In summary, many LGBT organizations will benefit from more diversity sexual orientation.

GENDER IDENTITY DIVERSITY

In 2007, the movement got a jolt when Representative Barney Frank said that he would strip transgender protections from his proposed Employment Nondiscrimination Act (ENDA) to enhance the chances of its quick passage—seven years later, ENDA has not yet passed. At that time, many prominent LGBT people and the Human Rights Campaign sided with Barney Frank. They said, "Why not pass protections for gays, lesbians, and bisexuals now and come back later with additional legislation for transgender people?" Many others said, "We are all in this together. We cannot leave our transgender friends behind." In just a few weeks, more than three hundred LGBT organizations signed up to push for an inclusive ENDA. A year later, Barney Frank reintroduced an inclusive ENDA. Finally, six months later, the Human Rights Campaign supported it.

Since then, in April 2012, the bipartisan Equal Employment Opportunity Commission decided unanimously that transgender and gender non-conforming individuals are protected from employment discrimination by Title VII of the Civil Rights Act.

Most LGBT organizations include transgender people in their programs. However, transgender people are not adequately represented in the governance of organizations in the movement. As of December 2013, the following twelve national LGBT organizations do not have a single transgender board member:

- Equality Forum

- Family Equality Council

- Freedom to Marry

- Gay and Lesbian Leadership Institute

- GroundSpark

- Immigration Equality

- Log Cabin Republicans

- Movement Advancement Project

- National Stonewall Democrats

- Outserve-SLDN

- Services and Advocacy for Gay, Lesbian, Bisexual and Transgender Elders (SAGE)

- The Trevor Project

Notably, the Human Rights Campaign, the largest LGBT organization, which has a forty-nine-member board, only has one transgender member.

Dr. Dana Beyer, an accomplished surgeon and transgender advocate, is leading a project of eQualityGiving to increase the number of transgender board members in the governing boards of organizations that represent LGBT people. An up-to-date list of transgender board members is available at: www.eQualityGiving.org/Transgender-Board-Members.

In 2012 progress was made: Lambda Legal added a transgender board member, Dr. Jillian Weiss, as did OutServe-SLDN, which appointed a transgender executive director, Allyson Robinson, who also served on the board. In 2013, the National Center for Lesbian Rights appointed Gareth Gill to its board and the Victory Fund appointed Matteus Stephens.

While agreeing on the need for a larger number of transgender board members, executive directors and board chairs provide the following justifications for such a lack of representation:

- *It is difficult to find candidates:* This is true; this is why Dr. Beyer's eQualityGiving project includes a list (with bios) of seventeen qualified transgender people who are willing to serve on national boards.

- *It is even more difficult to find candidates who can meet the financial requirements*: This is true, as some of these organizations expect their board members to contribute or fundraise tens of thousands of dollars every year. However, organizations should remember that the primary function of a board is governance, not fundraising (as most like to think). Organizations can always have another board charged with fundraising or waive or reduce fundraising requirements for some board members.

- *They already cover transgender people in their programs:* This is true in most organizations, but it is not a substitute for organizations that claim to represent lesbian, gay, bisexual, and transgender people to have them on their governing boards.

RACIAL DIVERSITY

The importance of racial diversity (including on boards) is well understood among LGBT organizations. Progress is occurring, but it is still slow. The experiences and needs of white, African-American, Latino, Asian, or Native-American LGBT Americans are different.

POLITICAL DIVERSITY

About 75 percent of LGBT Americans vote for democrats. This is one of the most solid and consistent voting blocks for the Democratic Party. Yet this party did not bring to a vote the Employment Nondiscrimination Act in 2009–10 while the party had the majority in the House and Senate.

It is important to acknowledge that a minority of LGBT people are Republicans. It is critical to ensure that legislators understand that LGBT equality is a nonpartisan issue. The Log Cabin Republicans work with the minority of Republican legislators who support some LGBT rights. Unfortunately, the majority of Republican legislators in Congress are strongly anti-equality. This is evidenced by their party platform, as well as by their votes against federal hate-crime legislation and repeal of "Don't Ask, Don't Tell."

ECONOMIC DIVERSITY

Much progress needs to occur in supporting the needs of LGBT people who are poor or destitute youth thrown out of the family's home or people with chronic diseases such as HIV who do not get appropriate medical care.

33.

Summary: Equal under the Law

A main foundation of American society is the belief that everybody should be treated equally under the law. This is same belief that is the essence of the gay agenda: to be treated equally under the law.

Here are the areas in which heterosexual, homosexual, bisexual, and transgender Americans are not yet treated the same under most states' laws and federal law:

- *Nondiscrimination in employment, housing, credit, public accommodation and facilities, and federally funded programs or activities:* Not treated equally at the federal level or in most states.

- *Marrying the person you love and having the freedom to live anywhere in the United States as a married couple:* Not achieved yet in most states.

- *A safe environment for all youth to learn without bullying and harassment*: Not achieved at the federal level or in most states.

- *Being able to be a parent and raise a family like everybody else:* Need federal legislation and additional legislation in most states.

- *Free to match your biological gender to your true gender:* Partially achieved.

- *Serving in the military without lying about who you are:* Achieved; *not being discriminated in the military due to your sexual orientation and gender identity:* Not achieved yet.

- *Hate-crime legislation:* Covered at the federal level but not covered in most states.

What paths can we take to be better and treat everybody equally under the law? The next chapters show the different ways.

Part III:

Different Paths?

34.

Three Main Paths

There are three main paths to reach legal equality:

1. Courts
2. Legislatures
3. Popular vote

The irony is people who want to deny the constitutional right of being equal under the law use the same paths to deny equality to people and even criminalize private, consenting behavior.

For instance, when confronted with a popular vote, the opponents of equality will make emotional, but false, appeals to "save the children." Or they will remind voters that marriage has been for 2,000 years between one man and one woman (which historically is not true). Or they will denounce the cost of unnecessary litigation if we are asking for non discrimination in employment. Or they will state that we are asking for special rights (which is not true, see chapter 16).

When legislators do want to limit our rights, they will pass legislation that has big exemptions. For instance, the courts in New Jersey granted full marriage equality in 2013. Some democratic legislators in the state now want to pass equal marriage legislation that has exemptions for religiously affiliated organizations.

When a court does not want to recognize the fundamental right to being equal, it will usually issue a ruling stating that the matter is to be decided by the legislature (knowing that legislatures, elected by majorities, have a hard time passing laws improving the lives of the minorities).

Another favored technique by opponents of equality is to go to court or to the legislature claiming that their freedom of religion is at stake, so they want to discriminate against others—in effect, *imposing* their religion on others. This is done not only about LGBT rights but also about family issues such as contraception.

Finally, when the courts grant equality, as required by the Constitution, opponents often label the judges as "activists" and seek to overturn their rulings by popular vote and even recall or impeach the judges.

In the past, in their disdain for some groups, such as African-Americans, opponents of equal rights went much further by going into a civil war and endangering the whole existence of our incipient nation. Many of these citizens who proclaimed to be for law and order would openly disregard court orders, such as for school integration. Or, worse yet, these citizens would take justice into their own hands, sometimes as part of supremacist organizations.

Fortunately, things are better now. We are not waging civil wars to settle our disagreements, but the willingness to keep some rights and protections only for the majority continues.

As a country, we are better than that. In the next chapters, let's review how the courts, the legislatures, and popular vote can be used to bring equality under the law to *all* Americans.

35.

Path #1: The Courts

In their brilliance, the Founding Fathers established a government system based on three *independent* branches. This independence among the branches is critical, especially for the legal rights of minorities. It is possible, but difficult, for minorities to get equal rights through legislation. This is because legislators, due to being elected by the majority, look first at legislation that affects the majority. They also may feel pressure from the majority to pass laws that marginalize unpopular minorities—such criminalizing what consenting adults do in the privacy of their bedrooms or legislating against interracial marriage, as they did in the past.

This is why the role of the courts is to be independent and focus on the Constitution and equality for all instead of the wishes of the majority. One of the most important Supreme Court decisions for treating LGBT people equally was *Lawrence v. Texas*, which, in 2003, struck down all the sodomy laws (which also affected heterosexuals). This was important because some people say that they do not oppose gays, just what they do in bed. Who are they to assume, much less judge, what consenting adults do in the privacy of their bedrooms?

Here is what the US Supreme Court had to say in its majority decision in *Lawrence v. Texas*:

> Liberty presumes an autonomy of self that includes freedom of thought, belief, expression, and certain intimate conduct.

> When sexuality finds overt expression in intimate conduct with another person, the conduct can be but one element in a personal bond that is more enduring. The liberty protected by the Constitution allows homosexual persons the right to make this choice.

> When homosexual conduct is made criminal by the law of the State, that declaration in and of itself is an invitation to subject *homosexual persons to discrimination both in the public and in the private spheres.*

In another important judicial decision, in 2004 the Massachusetts Supreme Judicial Court in *Goodridge v. Department of Public Health* acknowledged that there are different points of view regarding same-gender marriage:

> Many people hold deep-seated religious, moral, and ethical convictions that marriage should be limited to the union of one man and one woman, and that homosexual conduct is immoral. Many hold equally strong religious, moral, and ethical convictions that same-sex couples are entitled to be married, and that homosexual persons should be treated no differently than their heterosexual neighbors.

In the end, it comes down to individual autonomy and equality under the law. The court continued:

> Marriage is a vital social institution.
>
> A person who enters into an intimate, exclusive union with another of the same sex is arbitrarily deprived of membership in one of our community's most rewarding and cherished institutions. That exclusion is incompatible with the constitutional principles of respect for individual autonomy and equality under law.

So the courts acknowledge that there are differences of opinion, but show that *the respect for individual autonomy and equality under the law should trump anything else.* That is the key principle that unites us as Americans. Still, some say the ruling is wrong, that they are "activist" judges creating laws instead of just interpreting them. The next chapter carefully examines this concern.

36.

Activist Judges

Some people complain about judicial activism, which popularly means that judges "legislate from the bench." These people believe that judges are taking the power from the people's representatives to create new laws and rights where none exist in the Constitution.

Some judges would like the US Constitution to be read literally, as it was written more than two hundred years ago, as if the world had not changed in the last two centuries. For instance, the role of the president as commander-in-chief also applies to the air force, although planes are never mentioned in the Constitution. Also, fortunately, we no longer accept that any human being could be three-fifths of a person.

Most people complaining about activist judges are conservatives. This criticism is usually addressed from the right at judges who have supported the freedom of individuals to marry the person they love. The reality is that studies show that the US Supreme Court, headed by conservative John Roberts, has been the most "activist" in decades, including the controversial ruling in *Citizens United v. Federal Election Commission* (January 21, 2010), in which the Supreme Court ruled that Congress could not impose limits to financial contributions from corporations and unions. This was an expansion well beyond what the Constitution says (which is mute about the subject) and well beyond established precedents.

In fact, in *Citizens United*, the Supreme Court went well beyond the outcome the plaintiff was asking. This is extreme activism. Citizens United, represented by Ted Olson (who represented Bush in 2000 and won the presidency for him), only wanted a ruling that said that long movies showed on a pay-per-view channel did not constitute electioneering and should be allowed to be shown before an election. Olson specifically asked the court not to change precedent about campaign finance legislation. Breaking precedent, restraint, and moderation, the Supreme Court completely changed the financing of elections. (Check the article "Money Unlimited" by Jeffrey Toobin in the *New Yorker*, May 21, 2012.)

Some politicians, such as Newt Gingrich, have gone as far as to state that the president should send the police to arrest a judge to compel appearance in front of a congressional committee to justify his or her rulings (on MSNBC's *Face the Nation*, December 18, 2011). Mr. Gingrich's demand is an attack on American democracy.

American democracy is based on three *independent* branches of government. The president (executive branch) cannot order anybody to appear in front of Congress (legislative branch). Similarly, Congress cannot compel judges (judicial branch) to reverse their rulings. Certainly, Congress can create new laws that, if they are constitutional, can have the effect of reversing a ruling. What a sad state of affairs it is when a politician makes such an outrageous statement and tries to undermine our democracy so heavily.

When we use the term *activist judges*, we are in reality attacking the independence of the three branches of government. As we said before, the brilliance of American democracy is the separation of powers. Legislators, elected by majority, tend to write legislation that represents the interests of the majority that elected them. Sometimes this legislation unnecessarily hurts a minority. This is why we need the judicial branch that, at the federal level, is not subject to elections to ensure that the rights of the minority are protected. We should all agree to support the *key constitutional principle of independence of judges*.

Let's read next about what the US Supreme Court did for LGBT rights in 2013.

37.

Supreme Indecision

"The doctrine of 'separate but equal' has no place."

—*Brown v. Board of Education*, 1954

On the tenth anniversary, to the date, of issuing its historic *Lawrence v. Texas* decision, the US Supreme Court issued two more rulings that significantly advanced LGBT equality under the law. Although the rulings were considered great victories for the community, in reality they were very moderate and limited. The Supreme Court did not rule on critical issues.

The first case, known as *Hollingsworth v. Perry*, challenged the constitutionality of California's Proposition 8, which defined marriage as between one man and one woman. Fighting this battle was a legal dream team, headed by Ted Olson and David Boies— the attorneys whom Bush and Gore selected, respectively, to represent them in front of the Supreme Court in 2000 for the job of President of the United States. Both attorneys have been very successful in portraying that marriage is a conservative institution. Certainly Olson, who also served as solicitor general under George W. Bush, has the credibility in the Court to make such an assertion. The case was brought up by a new organization, the American Foundation for Equal Rights, which was heavily criticized by heads of national LGBT organizations for doing so under the reasoning that it was not the right time to go to the Supreme Court and that we could lose a lot with a ruling opposing equality.

The Court could have delivered a range of rulings: (1) declaring marriage a constitutional right available to all couples in every state of the union, or (2) deciding that the states with civil unions or domestic partnerships should convert them to marriage, or (3) ruling that California should allow same-gender marriages, or (4) determining that they should have never heard the case in any event (therefore allowing California to conduct same-gender marriages again), or (5) upholding Proposition 8 and therefore denying more same-gender couples in California to get married until Proposition 8 is overturned by the voters, or (6) avoiding a decision based on the technical issue of who has standing to bring this case to the Court. These were the six main options—there were, of course, a large number of variations that were also possible. The Court chose the last option, in effect not making a decision. In practice, though, this meant that the ruling from the Court of Appeals stood as legal. This meant that same-gender couples were able to resume marrying in California within days.

The second case, *United States v. Windsor,* was about the federal government not recognizing legal marriages. The case involved Edie Windsor and Thea Spyer who got engaged in 1967 and were not allowed to marry until forty years later in Canada. They lived in New York, which, at the time, did not offer marriage licenses to same-gender couples but recognized marriages from elsewhere. When Thea died in 2009, the federal government imposed a $363,000-estate tax. If the IRS had treated them as a married couple, there would be no tax at all. The US Supreme Court ruled that the IRS should refund the money and that Section 3 of the Defense of Marriage Act (DOMA) was unconstitutional. However, it left unchanged Section 2 of DOMA which allows states not to accept the same-gender marriage from another state.

This case not only brought to light significant financial discrimination ($363,000), but the wonderful love story of two women committed to each other for more than forty years. Edie Windsor reflected, months after the Supreme Court ruling, about her love story and wondered what their lives could have been if they did not have to hide who they were. How much more could they have contributed to society if they could have been open about who they were?

This case was successfully litigated by the American Civil Liberties Union.

The Obama administration took immediate action to fully implement the ruling. The result is that married same-gender couples who live in a state that allows such marriages have full marriage equality in front of the federal government, including veterans benefits, filing taxes as married, sponsoring the spouse for immigration, etc.

However, some federal laws are based on the state of domicile of the couple, not the location of the marriage (called "state of celebration"). This makes same-gender couples who travel or relocate to discriminatory states to be considered as not married by the federal government, suddenly losing important federal benefits they paid for, such as a survivor social security. In addition, such states would treat the couple as not married.

A positive consequence of this Supreme Court ruling was that it clearly showed that civil unions are not the same as marriage. Even if a state considered them the same except for the word marriage, the federal government does not consider people in a civil union as married. This helped persuade the legislatures of Illinois and Hawai'i to change their civil unions statutes to full marriage equality. Undoubtably, this will have an effect in future marriage battles in other states.

The majority opinion was written by Justice Kennedy, who stated:

> DOMA's unusual deviation from the usual tradition of recognizing and accepting state definitions of marriage here operates to deprive same-sex couples with the benefits and responsibilities that come with the federal recognition of their marriages. This is strong evidence of a law having the purpose and effect of disapproval of that class. The avowed purpose and practical effect of the law here in question are to impose a disadvantage, a separate status, and so a stigma upon all who enter into same-sex marriages made lawful by the unquestioned authority of the States.

Justice Kennedy ten years earlier to the date wrote the ground breaking decision of *Lawrence v. Texas,* which decriminalized private, consensual sex and overturned in full a prior decision of the US Supreme Court, *Bowers v. Hardwick,* which was openly discriminatory towards LGBT people.

Justice Alito wrote in a dissent:

> Same-sex marriage presents a highly emotional and important question of public policy—but not a difficult question of constitutional law. The Constitution does not guarantee the right to enter

into a same-sex marriage. Indeed, no provision of the Constitution speaks to the issue.

This statement is outrageous since the Constitution does not address marriage at all (much less whether marriage is between one man and one woman). This has not stopped the Supreme Court from ruling in other cases that marriage is a fundamental right.

Justice Scalia in his dissent expressed his expectation that the Supreme Court will rule for full marriage equality in the future:

> In my opinion, however, the view that this Court will take of state prohibition of same-sex marriage is indicated beyond mistaking by today's opinion. As I have said, the real rationale of today's opinion, whatever disappearing trail of its legalistic argle-bargle one chooses to follow, is that DOMA is motivated by bare desire to harm couples in same-sex marriages. How easy it is, indeed how inevitable, to reach the same conclusion with regard to state laws denying same-sex couples marital status.

Justice Scalia is totally right. Within the next few years the Court will be faced with multiple cases regarding same-sex marriage and, if the Court does not become more conservative, the ruling shall be to allow same-gender marriage across the United States.

When considering marriage equality, one needs to remember *Loving v. Virginia*, the landmark Supreme Court unanimous ruling that allowed interracial marriages across the United States in 1967. This is a ruling worth reading because of its clarity and brevity (less than five pages). It concludes:

> The Fourteenth Amendment requires that the freedom of choice to marry not be restricted by invidious racial discriminations. Under our Constitution, the freedom to marry, or not marry, a person of another race resides with the individual, and cannot be infringed by the State.

This precedent should remind Justice Alito what he certainly knows: the Fourteenth Amendment does not mention marriage at all, just *"equal protection of the laws"* which is precisely what LGBT people want, the gay agenda.

The concurring decision from Justice Stewart in the *Loving v. Virginia* case is even briefer and stated in its entirety:

> I have previously expressed the belief that "it is simply not possible for a state law to be valid under our Constitution which makes the criminality of an act depend upon the race of the actor." McLaughlin v. Florida, 379 U.S. 184, 198 (concurring opinion). Because I adhere to that belief, I concur in the judgment of the Court.

On the fortieth anniversary of *Loving v. Virginia,* Mildred Loving stated:

> I believe all Americans, no matter their race, no matter their sex, no matter their sexual orientation, should have that same freedom to marry. Government has no business imposing some people's religious beliefs over others. Especially if it denies people's civil rights.

Although the two LGBT equality decisions of the Supreme Court in 2013 were favorable, they were incomplete. Furthermore, the Windsor case could have produced another critical outcome beyond federal recognition of marriages: it could have imposed the *heightened scrutiny standard* for court decisions. Under this standard, the government would have to justify the reasons for any discrimination against LGBT people. This would immensely help achieve all the equality goals.

The next chapters discuss the role of the legislatures for achieving equality.

38.

Path #2: The Legislatures

"The establishment and guardianship of full civil
rights is a non-partisan issue."

—The Dallas Principles,
Principle #5

In order to have legislation enacted that treats minorities equally under the law, we need to:

1. Support the election (and reelection) of legislators who are pro-equality. We need to support these candidates independently of their party affiliations (although most are Democrats) and their sexual orientation (many of our biggest supporters are heterosexual).

2. Follow up after the election to ensure that these legislators introduce and support pro-equality legislation.

3. Persuade other legislators to vote for equality legislation. The more they get to know gay, lesbian, bisexual, and transgender constituents, the more they understand their personal plight, the more they support pro-equality legislation.

The next five chapters present practical approaches regarding legislative activism.

39.

Endorsing Candidates for Elected Office

"Those who seek our support are expected to
commit to these principles."

—The Dallas Principles,
Principle #8

In the summer of 2012, the Democratic Party adopted a platform that for the first time was fully pro-equality (the Green Party has had such a platform for many years). Despite that, as many as twenty percent of the Democratic senators did not support it fully as late as 2013. Through intense lobbying, nowadays one can expect that all future candidates from the Democratic Party will be fully pro-equality. This radically changes how to endorse candidates.

First, as we said in prior editions of the *Gay Agenda,* there is no reason to support (financially or by volunteering) any candidate, from either party, who is not fully pro-equality.

Second, there is now not much point in endorsing in the primaries because in the Democratic Party all the candidates in a race are likely to be pro-equality. If the Republican Party has a pro-equality candidate, then he or she will probably face a pro-equality democrat in the general election.

Multiple organizations endorse candidates under different criteria. For example, the Victory Fund only endorses candidates who are lesbian, gay, bisexual, or transgender. The presence of LGBT legislators is important in the dialog that ensues with other legislators, beyond equality issues. Furthermore, LGBT legislators can help their colleagues understand the impact of their equality votes and have been effective in passing equality legislation. However, there are heterosexual legislators who have been more supportive on equality issues than their LGBT counterparts. For Congress, in the short term, what we need to achieve full equality is control of the House and the Senate by the Democratic Party, since the Republican Party is not bringing for a vote pro-equality legislation. (To the credit of the Republican leadership, in the last session of Congress they have not brought the Federal Marriage Amendment up for a vote.)

Another organization, Log Cabin Republicans, supports only Republican candidates, but, contrary to the Victory Fund, they endorse independently of sexual orientation. They endorse candidates who are partly pro-equality, since few republicans are fully pro-equality.

The Human Rights Campaign also issues an endorsement list, although the criteria used are unknown.

eQualityGiving, the organization that my spouse and I founded in 2005, endorses candidates who support all the equality goals— regardless of party affiliation or sexual orientation or gender identity. The current focus is on *Critical Equality Races;* these are races which meet the following criteria: (1) one candidate is fully pro-equality while the other is anti-equality, (2) the race is close, and (3) the extra funding can make a difference. As stated before, the best bang for the buck in 2014 is in the general elections, instead of the primaries.

To achieve equality, we need to support pro-equality candidates— but all the money invested does not matter if the votes are not counted accurately. We are still not very good at counting votes, as the next chapter discusses

40.

Counting the Votes

If you are investing heavily in politics, either with your money or your time, you should support legislation at the state and federal levels to ensure the auditability of elections and unobstructed voter registration and voting. The problems of the 2000 election have not been corrected, all the contrary.

In November 2000, Americans learned a very important lesson about the most fundamental right in a democracy: the ability to accurately and verifiably determine who the people have voted to represent them.

That presidential election illustrated a series of problems:

- Unreliable machines that left punch cards with hanging chads

- Butterfly ballots that confused voters

- Bullies banging on the doors of the recount offices, intimidating and forcing to stop the recount

- The limitations of the electoral college as a way to choose a president

- The fact that the presidential election was not decided by 537 votes in Florida but by just one vote in the Supreme Court

The 2000 presidential election showed that each vote makes a difference. What has happened, then, in the last thirteen years to improve our elections?

In October 2002, by a bipartisan vote, Congress approved the Help America Vote Act (HAVA). This legislation has a very significant flaw: it funded the elimination of punch-card and lever machines while recommending that they be replaced by direct recording electronic (DRE) voting machines that cannot be audited. The good news is that there will be no more hanging chads; the bad news is that, wherever paperless DREs are used, there is no way now to verify the voter's intentions.

In early 2005, the Democratic National Committee established a commission (of which I was appointed a member) to analyze whether there was fraud in Ohio in the presidential election of 2004. My research discovered the solution to one of the biggest problems in any election: how to audit the aggregation of the results from each voting station to form the final count for a district or a state. My solution got much attention and was codified into legislation introduced by Dr. Rush Holt, a rocket scientist, who is the member of Congress representing the Princeton area and who is the foremost expert in Congress on election law.

Congressman Rush Holt has introduced multiple times a number of bills pertaining specifically to protecting the accuracy, integrity, and security of the vote count. His Voter Confidence and Increased Accessibility Act (introduced first in 2003) would have established requirements and provided funding for verifiable elections using paper ballots and routine random audits, similar to his Emergency Assistance for Secure Elections Act (introduced in 2008). Two additional pieces of legislation, the Vote Tabulation Audit Act (introduced first in 2006) and the Poll Tape Transparency Act (introduced first in 2008), both based on my ideas, would have provided for a transparent and verifiable aggregation of vote tallies.

Although all of these pieces of legislation have been pending in several successive Congresses, only the Voter Confidence and Increased Accessibility Act and the Emergency Assistance for Secure Elections Act were ever reported by committee, and only the Emergency Assistance for Secure Elections Act ever received a floor vote. It did receive a majority of support, but it was brought to the floor under a procedural rule requiring a supermajority. The Bush Administration circulated a statement of policy against the legislation before the vote, and it failed to receive the supermajority required. Neither bill was brought again to the floor, even though various versions of each had earned a majority of cosponsors in the House. Not passing new voting legislation has been a big misstep by the Democratic Party.

Meanwhile, the Republican Party has been very proactive and successful in passing legislation in several states to make it more difficult for individuals to register to vote and cast their vote. They claim that the purpose of this type of legislation is to ensure that only citizens vote—but this is a false argument since the number of non-citizens voting is extremely small or zero (for example, in a lawsuit in Pennsylvania, the state could not show a single case of non-citizens voting). The real aim of that legislation is to make it more difficult for certain groups of citizens to vote: seniors, minorities, poor people, and college students. These are groups that tend to vote Democrat.

The best reports on the impact of recent changes to voter registration and voter identification laws are *Voting Law Changes in 2012*, *The Challenge of Obtaining Voter Identification*, and *State Restrictions on Voter Registration Drives*, which are available for free downloading at www.brennancenter.org.

The real issue is the auditability of elections. The best report on auditability and preparedness is *Counting Votes 2012: A State by State Look at Voting Technology Preparedness*, which is available for free downloading at www.countingvotes.org.

Good organizations working on voting include the following:

- Verified Voting (www.verifiedvoting.org)

- Brennan Center for Justice at New York University Law School (www.brennancenter.org)

- Common Cause Education Fund (www.commoncause.org)

- Advancement Project (www.advancementproject.org)

- Election Protection Coalition (www.866ourvote.org)

In 2000, counting the votes became all-important because of an activist Supreme Court, which decided the presidential election by one vote. After 2010, counting the money is all-important thanks to an activist Supreme Court, which changed the role of money in elections by one vote.

The next chapter further investigates money's role in elections.

41.

Counting the Money

Money has always played a role in politics. However, in 2010, the US Supreme Court elevated the role of money in politics to new heights when it ruled in a five to four decision that corporations and unions can spend unlimited amounts of money on political electioneering communications, including advocating for the election or defeat of candidates (*Citizens United v. Federal Election Commission*). The conservative majority of the Supreme Court also decided that such unlimited expenditures do not constitute "a risk of corruption or the appearance of corruption."

Who are they kidding?

Justice Stevens explained in his dissent:

> At bottom, the Court's opinion is thus a rejection of the common sense of the American people, who have recognized a need to prevent corporations from undermining self government since the founding, and who have fought against the distinctive corrupting potential of corporate electioneering since the days of Theodore Roosevelt.

This was a major activist decision, breaking precedent and not giving due deference to Congress (which had imposed limitations on such expenditures). This is exactly the opposite of the restraint that Chief Justice Roberts claimed during his confirmation hearings.

It gets worse: two months after that decision, the Federal Court of Appeals for the DC circuit ruled on the case of *Speechnow.org v. FEC*.

The result of both decisions is the creation a new entity: super PACs, which can raise *unlimited amounts of money* from corporations, unions, other groups, and individuals, and they do *not* need to disclose the identity of the donors. They have some trivial limitations: they cannot coordinate with a campaign and cannot make direct financial contributions to campaigns. but they can pay for their own advertisements, even targeting specific candidates.

The US Supreme Court is expected to rule in 2014 in the case of *McCutcheon v. Federal Election Commission*. This is a case that seeks to remove any limits on the amounts individuals can give to candidates and political parties.

The are only two main solutions to limit the influence of big money on our democracy. The first one is to wait for the appointment of more liberal judges. The second one is an amendment to the Constitution, which is very difficult; one of the organizations working on this is FreeSpeechForPeople.org.

42.

They Were Wrong

"Those who attempt to divide our community or to
delay and deny action on civil equality, waiting for
the right moment to arrive, will be held
accountable."

—Preamble to the Dallas Principles

Several well-known LGBT people in prominent positions called for
not taking risks before the 2012 election, as they had done in prior
elections. The argument was that if President Obama was to come
out in favor of marriage equality or even sign a nondiscrimination
executive order, he could lose some of the swing states and then
lose the election.

By now we know that they were wrong. The president did come
out strongly in support of marriage equality, won nine of the ten
swing states, and won reelection. Furthermore, all four states that
had marriage equality ballot referenda voted in favor of marriage
equality, whereas the issue had lost relentlessly in the past without
the President's support.

Why is it important to highlight this? Not because those political
leaders are evil or ill-intentioned. On the contrary, most of them
are highly intelligent (some educated in some of the best
universities in the world) and well-meaning. They will tell you that
they spoke in their personal capacities. However, the press,
Congress, and the White House saw them as the leaders of the
LGBT movement (even if they may not consider themselves so).
What they were saying had impact. So, we need to highlight when
they were wrong.

One cannot lead from behind or continue with the same strategies
that did not work. The true leaders of the movement are those who
are in front, those who propose new ideas, those who think bigger.
The following chapters illustrate such a change in approaches.

43.

Insiders and Outsiders

For years, the politics of LGBT equality have been played as an insiders' and outsiders' game—the insiders being open LGBT elected officials, people with positions within the administration or the Democratic Party, or people in certain LGBT organizations (or those who wanted to be in those positions one day); every body else were outsiders.

When asked about LGBT equality, insiders would suggest for the most part, small, incremental advances and provide a rationale for why this was not the right time to move forward to fully reach equality, as discussed in the prior chapter. With the release of the Dallas Principles, which asks for full equality now, those insiders would say that they believed in equality, but that this was just not the right time.

The outsiders, in the meantime, would criticize the slow progress in achieving equality and would demand more advances right away.

The game would then be played in which astute insiders would point out to the demands of the outsiders and would make requests for more advances (while explaining that they understood the difficult position that the administration or Congress faced).

The first thing that some insiders would do would be to change the demands from the outsiders into requests—most insiders hate the word "demands." The second thing was to provide cover for the decisions made by the administration or Congress since LGBT "leaders" had been consulted. Of course, leadership is not measured by position but by vision and the capability to be in front of (not behind) the needs of those led and to possess the skills to get the job done.

The game needs to change now. It is time for insiders to be in unison with outsiders and demand to achieve full equality now. Without delays. Without excuses.

44.

Politics As the Art of the Possible

"Rethink Possible."

—AT&T marketing slogan

In the last few years, the buzzword sentence among politicians has been: "Politics is the art of the possible." It may sound like a reasonable approach, especially when you have Congress and the presidency divided among the two main political parties. But, who defines what is possible?

Emphasizing what is possible is thinking in transactional terms in a world that needs transformational thinking.

The possible is the art of mediocrity, which is exactly the opposite of what America is all about. We are creators, innovators, frontier-seekers. President Kennedy did not ask, "Is it possible to put a man on the moon?" It was an impossible dream, but he led us to the moon. President Johnson did not ask, "Is it possible to pass the Civil Rights Act?" He did not have the votes, but he got the bill passed. President Lincoln did not ask, "Is it possible to pass the Thirteenth Amendment?" All his advisors told him it was not possible and the leaders of Congress told him that he did not have the votes. Lincoln did pass the Thirteenth Amendment regardless that the war was about to end (and, with it, his major leverage). More recently, in 2011, Governor Cuomo did not ask, "Is it possible to pass marriage equality with a state senate controlled by the Republican party?" He just did it.

As the AT&T slogan says, it is time to "Rethink Possible."

If anybody tells you that "politics is the art of the possible," suggest that we find true leaders.

45.

More Republicans Are In

> "Let me take the pro-gay marriage people and the religious people—I believe that there is a connecting dot there that nobody is looking at, and that's the Constitution. The question is not whether gay people should be married or not. The question is why is the government involved in our marriage?"
>
> —Glenn Beck, December 10, 2012

Certainly, it is welcome that Glenn Beck sees the connection between our freedoms and the Constitution—which was the basis of *The Gay Agenda 2012,* and its successors now in its third year, which presumably he has not read yet.

Like Glenn Beck, more and more conservatives are "in" and understand that less government means that the government should not interfere with the freedom of people to marry the person they love, including same-gender partners. So it is not surprising that an increasing number of Republican voters support marriage equality, as well as quite a few influential Republican leaders:

- Dick Cheney, former vice president

- Rob Portman, US senator representing Ohio

- Lisa Murkowski, US senator representing Alaska

- Mark Kirk, US senator representing Illinois

- Laura Bush, former first lady

- Nancy Reagan, former first lady

- David Koch, a billionaire who, with his brother Charles, has given a record $400 million to Republican candidates in the 2012 election cycle

- Paul Singer, a billionaire hedge fund manager who donated millions to pass marriage equality legislation in New York in 2010 and several other states in 2012

- Jon Huntsman, former Governor of Utah and Republican presidential candidate in 2012

- Gary Johnson, former governor of New Mexico, who was the 2012 presidential candidate from the Libertarian Party

- General Colin Powell, former secretary of state

- Ken Mehlman, former chairman of the National Republican Committee as well as the campaign manager for George W. Bush's reelection campaign

- Meg Whitman, former candidate for California governor, who opposed marriage equality during her candidacy

- Cindy McCain and Meghan McCain, wife and daughter of presidential candidate John McCain

- Christine Todd Whitman, former governor of New Jersey

- William Weld, former governor of Massachusetts

- Jane Swift, former governor of Massachusetts

- Carlos Gutierrez, secretary of commerce under George W. Bush

- Steve Schmidt, McCain's presidential campaign manager in 2008

- David Blankenhorn, founder and president of the Institute for American Values, who wrote *The Future of Marriage,* a 2007 book *opposing* gay marriage

- Newt Gingrich, while not coming out for same-gender marriage yet, was quoted by *The Huffington Post* on

December 20, 2012, as saying: "[Gingrich] suggested that the party (and he himself) could accept a distinction between a 'marriage in a church from a legal document issued by the state'—the latter being acceptable."

- George H.W. Bush, without making a statement of support for marriage equality attended a wedding of two women in Maine in 2013...and signed the marriage certificate as an official witness.

Several of these individuals are not only expressing support or donating money, but are forming organizations or modifying the mission of their organizations to achieve LGBT legal equality.

However, we need to understand that several of these individuals have simultaneously supported the campaigns of politicians who are committed anti-equality zealots. This conflict is less pronounced when these individuals spend their money funding their own organizations, but when they fund a progressive organization, it forces the organization to examine the bigger picture of accepting money from sources that also fund candidates actively opposed to our equality under the law.

The help we need from Republican leaders now is to change the minds of the leadership in the House of Representatives to allow a vote on LGBT issues and free their members to vote their consciences instead of a party line—not only for marriage equality but also for all the equality goals still pending. The rules in the House of Representatives are such that the consent of the House leadership is required to bring legislation to a vote, even if the majority of it supports it. At the same time, the Democrats need to ensure that all the members of their caucus support full equality now. The votes we are seeking from Congress are about each of the equality goals, not just marriage.

46.

From Endorsements to Legislation: Act on Principles

Endorsing candidates who are pro-equality is critical for achieving equality under the law. Therefore, we have to ensure that they win despite unlimited and secret financing and although in most states there is no way to audit the results of the election, because of the use of electronic voting machines with no verifiable paper trails.

If, despite all of these obstacles, a pro-equality candidate wins, it is time to get into action—we need to ensure that pro-equality legislators introduce legislation that will bring full legal equality to all Americans. To do so, there is a powerful internet tool: Act On Principles (www.ActOnPrinciples.org), which lists all the federal pro-equality legislation that has been introduced in Congress and identifies how each member of Congress is expected to vote on it. This tool also allows any interested party to update the vote count with any new information. Furthermore, web masters can insert a widget in their sites that keeps the up-to-the-minute vote count.

All parties in Congress and state legislatures use whip counts, which is asking the members of their party how they plan to vote on a piece of legislation. This helps the party leadership determine what to introduce for a vote. Lobbyists also keep their own private whip counts (covering both parties) to determine candidates who need to be persuaded. Whip counts have always been a very closely guarded secret. This new tool makes whip counts open and transparent—quite a revolution. Now there is a simple way to track legislation. This tool was created and is funded by this author; Donald Hitchcock updates the website.

In the last few chapters, we have talked about achieving legal equality through legislation. What about losing rights by popular vote? Isn't voting the essence of democracy? The next chapter addresses these crucial questions and more.

47.

Path #3: Popular Vote

"Religious beliefs are not a basis upon which to
affirm or deny civil rights."

—The Dallas Principles,
Principle #4

This is a democracy; let's all vote!

Certainly, voting is a critical part of a democracy. However, should
we vote on fundamental rights? How would you like it if people
had a vote on whether *you* have the right to marry? Let's take the
case that the person you love is from a different race. Should you
have the right to marry? Should we take a vote on this?

In 1967, when the Supreme Court decided that interracial
marriage should be legal, 72 percent of Americans were opposed
to it (source: www.religioustolerance.org/hom_mar14.htm).

In November 2000, there was a vote in Alabama to eliminate from
their statutes the prohibition against interracial marriage. Only 60
percent of voters in Alabama agreed to that removal, despite that
the Supreme Court made it illegal to forbid interracial marriages
for thirty-three years before that vote.

As recently as in March 2011, a poll of Republicans voters in
Mississippi revealed that 46 percent of them believe that you
should not have the right to marry somebody of a different race
(source: www.religioustolerance.org/hom_mar14.htm).

So, was it an activist Supreme Court that allowed interracial
marriages? In fact, the Constitution is silent about interracial
marriages (as it is about any marriages). Actually, when the
Constitution was enacted, interracial marriage was forbidden in
most states. Fortunately, the Supreme Court in 1967 saw their job
as being *independent*. They understood that even if a very large

majority of Americans were opposed to interracial marriage, they could not deny the fundamental right of a person to marry the person they love. Also fortunately, we did not take a vote in 1967 about whether interracial marriage should be legal. Clearly it would have lost. The lesson, of course, is that we *cannot put the rights of a minority to a majority vote.*

We have examined so far the three main paths to win (or lose) equality: the courts, the legislatures, and the popular vote. The next chapter will examine other strategies that apply to each of these three main paths.

48.

Winning Hearts and Minds

Whether you follow the path of the courts, the legislatures, or popular votes, a key component for each of them is to win the hearts and minds of the American people, the judges, and the elected officials.

Organizations like GLAAD (glaad.org) have worked very hard for decades to change hearts and minds through the media, and have been joined by other organizations such as EqualityMatters.org. Popular TV shows and movies have helped Americans understand better that there are lesbian, gay, bisexual, and transgender individuals in all occupations, and that, at the end of the day, we are all the same—we are all human beings with our accomplishments, strengths, weaknesses, and needs.

If you are an LGBT person in the closet, the most effective step that you can take to win hearts and minds is to come out to friends, family, coworkers, and everybody. Increasingly more people are accepting and embracing, but it really depends on many factors. Most of your friends and family may already suspect anyway.

If you cannot endure coming out of the closet or you believe that you are not gay or lesbian or bisexual despite having sex with somebody of the same gender, at least show respect for LGBT people by not tolerating homophobic jokes, by supporting equality policies in your workplace, and by voting for equality if you are an elected official.

You can express your support for equality in every day-to-day conversation—even with strangers. You can be an activist tourist and make clear to hotel staff, taxi drivers, shopkeepers, and others that you are LGBT and why you are visiting their town.

The most important minds to change are those of the people who can change the minds of many others. For instance, whenever you are in front of an elected official, you can always preface any conversation by saying something as short as, "Please pass LGBT equality legislation now," like a female service member who whispered to President Obama, "Please repeal 'Don't Ask, Don't Tell.'" This is what this author did when invited to the White House in 2009. I told the president, the first lady, the vice president, the second lady, and my senator the importance of full LGBT equality. I also handed a letter to President Obama that said, in its entirety (with the italics and bold as in the original):

May 4, 2009

Dear President Obama,

Thank you for taking a moment to read this letter from a gay American.

I came to this country twenty-nine years ago with a Fulbright fellowship when America was the beacon of freedom. I got a doctorate from Stanford University, reached financial success, and retired at age forty. I became a citizen and lived the American dream.

But now America is no longer the leader in civil rights, as gay couples are not treated equally, like they are in many countries, including my former one, Spain.
Many American politicians are following your lead in a call for civil unions, a separate and unequal institution. You continue to express publicly your personal belief that marriage is between a man and a woman—which is clearly discriminatory and contrary to the practice of many religions, including your own.

When you say that you believe marriage is between a man and a woman, please know that those words feel like <u>a knife going through our hearts.</u> It is hurtful to us every time you say that, and it is harmful to our struggle for equal rights.

It would be helpful if you would instead say something like the following:

"As President, it is my duty to make sure all Americans are treated equally.

Our country is deeply divided on this issue.

*Some states allow same-gender marriage, some civil unions and domestic partnerships, and some states forbid it in their state constitutions. **The federal government needs to recognize and treat equally all marriage licenses issued by a state.***

*Marriage is also a religious institution. Since the US Constitution states that 'Congress shall make no law respecting an establishment of religion, or prohibiting the free exercise thereof,' **rest assured that the federal government will not interfere with religions' right to marry who they want. Some religions perform same-gender marriages, and other religions forbid it."***

I am available to discuss this matter with you or your aides at any time.

Sincerely,

Juan Ahonen-Jover, Ph.D.

Three years and four days after getting this letter, President Obama came out in favor of marriage equality. This letter is just one example of the combined effort of thousands of people who made it possible: we won the hearts and minds not only of the American people but of the president of the United States.

49.

Equal Rights and Businesses

"IF YOU DON'T LIKE GAY MARRIAGE,
DON'T GET GAY MARRIED."

—Billboard advertisement for Manhattan Mini
Storage

While awaiting federal and state legislation to provide nondiscrimination, we need to rely on policies adopted voluntarily by businesses. Since 2002, the Human Rights Campaign has kept a Corporate Equality Index; Appendix 3 lists companies with a rating of 100 percent. This index shows tremendous progress by American corporations: 110 of the top Fortune 500 corporations have a perfect rating of 100 percent in 2013 (up from eighty-eight in 2012), and thirteen of the top twenty corporations in America reach the same perfect rating. Still, legislation to protect against nondiscrimination is badly needed since the Fortune 500 employs only a small part of the workforce in the United States.

Note that an executive order from the president requiring that all federal contractors do not discriminate in employment based on sexual orientation or gender identity or expression would immediately cover almost 20 percent of the working population in the United States. Such an executive order is ready for President Obama's signature. He indicated that he would not sign it until after the 2012 election. So, the time is overdue.

A good example of a company being pro-active about equality is Google, which, in 2012, launched a worldwide campaign called Legalize Love. It is about full LGBT equality, not just marriage. It focuses on countries with a homophobic culture and countries that punish being LGBT.

Another good example is Marriott, which recently joined a coalition to fight the Defense of Marriage Act. Marriott was founded by a Mormon, and his son, Bill Marriott, also a devout Mormon, is the executive chairman. While Bill Marriott personally believes that marriage is between one man and one woman, and he does not drink alcohol, he recently stated, "Our church is very much opposed to alcohol and we're probably one of the biggest sales engines of liquor in the United States. I don't drink. We serve a lot of liquor." He also stated, "We have all the American values: the values of hard work, the values of integrity, the values of fairness and respect." Indeed, these are the values of America and any good business.

A poignant video called *Find Your Understanding* was created by Expedia, the online travel company. It has been watched more than 2.6 million times. It is a wonderful example of a corporation understanding human nature. Watch it at www.youtube.com/watch?v=ThzdsnXeE28

A new issue has surfaced after the *Citizens United* decision by the Supreme Court in 2010: corporations can donate *unlimited* amounts of money for electioneering, and they can do so *anonymously*. For instance, a corporation may be giving to elect conservative candidates to lower corporate tax rates or reduce regulation of an industry. Given that most fiscally conservative candidates are nowadays also socially conservative, the corporations may be giving to candidates who legislate against equality. A corporation may even have a 100-percent rating in the Corporate Equality Index and may even donate to an LGBT nonprofit—while at the same time support candidates who are anti-equality.

To solve this problem requires external pressure as well as inside advocates (in which OutAndEqual.org and employee LGBT groups play a key role). This represents one of the most important and unresolved issues facing our relationship with corporations. It is also a difficult problem to resolve because corporate giving for electioneering can be impossible to track since it can be done anonymously.

In the 2012 elections, some corporations, supported by the *Citizens United* decision, took the unprecedented step of sending their employees "voting guides" or letters from the CEO asking all the employees to support certain candidates. For example, Wynn Resorts, which is the third-largest casino company in the country, sent such a voting guide to its twelve thousand employees asking them to vote for conservative candidates—many of whom are anti-equality. Note, ironically, that Wynn Resorts has a 100-percent rating in the Corporate Equality Index from the Human Rights Campaign.

50.

Building Coalitions

Not to state the obvious, but work to reach equality requires building coalitions. We need to:

- Work with the women's political community since it is a big supporter of the LGBT community. In the four states in which marriage equality was on the ballot in November 2012, women supported us more than men. In Maine, it was 61 percent of women in favor versus 47 percent of men. In Washington State, 57 percent of women were in favor versus 49 percent of men. In Maryland, the vote was 55 percent of women versus 48 percent of men. In Minnesota, the tally was 56 percent of women versus 46 percent of men. None of the four ballot initiatives would have passed if only men had voted.

- Demonstrate to the African-American community that the LGBT community truly understands its issues, its cultures, and its religious heritages, and that our organizations are truly diverse.

- Help the immigrant communities that, like LGBT people, want to be full US citizens and not second-class ones.

- Continue supporting the disability community, as they have supported the LGBT community.

- Ensure that governing boards for LGBT organizations include gay and lesbian and bisexual and transgender board members.

- Encourage Republican voters to support equality. In the ballot initiative for marriage in Maryland in November 2012, in many Republican precincts, marriage equality won a majority despite that President Obama did not carry the precinct.

- Show businesses that LGBT customers are indeed loyal to companies that support equality.

- Demonstrate every day to employers that LGBT employees perform excellently in their jobs.

The following chapter summarizes what we've learned in Part III.

51.

Summary: The Paths to Equality

We have seen that there are three main paths to legal equality:

1. *Courts*
   This is the most cost-effective way. We discussed the real meaning of activist judges and why the current conservative Supreme Court is very much activist.

2. *Legislatures*
   It is key to have a high-quality and transparent process for endorsing candidates and then to follow up after the election to ensure that legislation is introduced, supported, and passed.

3. *Popular Vote*
   Putting the rights of a minority up to a vote of the majority is clearly the easiest way to lose equality instead of achieving it, but over time the majority will support marriage equality in some states.

In addition, for any of the main paths to equality, we need to continue winning hearts and minds and building coalitions.

We also discussed the newest issue in our relationship with businesses: some companies are very good with LGBT employees and customers while, at the same time, helping elect anti-equality legislators who vote or legislate against our rights.

We have examined formal paths to equality. In the next chapters, we'll explore what path *you* can take to make a difference.

Part IV:

What You Can Do In 2014

52.

Don't Stop

"Full civil rights for lesbian, gay, bisexual and
transgender individuals must be enacted now.
Delay and excuses are no longer acceptable."

—The Dallas Principles,
Principle #1

How long to continue your LGBT activism is a very personal
decision; some people may have reached the point of taking a rest.
Their reasons usually fall into two categories: (1) the momentum
in the last two years has been so great that equality is now
unstoppable, "it will happen anyway" or (2) we have reached full
equality in my state, so "I am done."

These are valid reasons. Yes, we may have reached the tipping
point. For years, the vast majority of Americans had indicated
their support for gays in the military as well as nondiscrimination
in employment. In 2013, a slight majority of Americans supported
that LGBT people should be able to marry. Despite all of that, the
real results are not so impressive: we can serve in the military
openly, but we are still not protected against discrimination in the
military, or in other employment. Furthermore, the president has
yet to sign an executive order to protect LGBT people working for
federal contractors (which is 20 percent of all employment). Also,
while the 2013 Supreme Court rulings were portrayed as a huge
victory for marriage equality, it was actually *Supreme Indecision*
(see chapter 37). More yet: while you might be fully equal in your
state (including marriage equality), you lose these protections
when you travel or relocate to *most* states of the Union.

Only four states and the District of Columbia offer full legal
equality. More than half the states still have an equality rating of
less than 50% in eQualityGiving's state scorecard.

At the federal level, eQualityGiving's Federal Equality Index has improved from 15 percent in 2012 to a still paltry 27 percent in 2013.

This is not the time to give up the fight, for three main reasons.

First, too many people are suffering and will continue to suffer until discriminatory laws are repealed and equality legislation is in place. They suffer because their relationships are not recognized. They suffer because they can be fired for being gay. They suffer bullying and much more. Their children suffer because their parents' marriage is not recognized everywhere. They are not asking anything that will cost the government money (in fact, studies show that allowing same-gender couples to marry saves the government money and enhances the state's economy). They are not asking for legislation that is difficult to create: simply update the laws that mention race, gender, national origin, and religion by adding the words *sexual orientation and gender identity.*

Second, the victories we had in 2012 and 2013, especially related to marriage equality and nondiscrimination in several states, did not happen by chance. The victories were hard won by carefully researching different types of messaging, by going door to door to voters based on research on how to approach different people about marriage, by intense lobbying of state legislatures, and by careful (and expensive) preparation for decisions in the courts, including the US Supreme Court. This was only possible through the generosity of so many donors and the work of staff and volunteers.

Third, there are plenty of periods in history in which there has been a backlash against acceptance of minorities. It can happen again very quickly as a charismatic leader or a popular celebrity could lead the country *backward.*

For LGBT activists, donors and supporters, this is not the time to take a break. This is the time to go all out and work for full equality now.

One of the actions that could be taken is to introduce legislation all at once that will make LGBT people equal under the law. The preferred method is by introduction of an omnibus bill, but if legislators do not want to take this path, then at least they should introduce separate bills covering all the inequalities; introducing all the bills the same day can increase the impact and support.

This author has proposed this strategy in prior editions of the *Gay Agenda*. The Republican Party won't do it, as most of its members are anti-equality. The Democratic Party has not done it because most democrats lack the fortitude to act on principles.

This is not the time to stop volunteering and giving. We are really close to getting full legal equality—but it won't happen without our collective, intensive, and creative work.

Let's get this job done.

53.

Your Turn: Eleven Actions *You* Can Take in 2014

"Individual involvement and grassroots action are
paramount to success and must be encouraged."

—The Dallas Principles,
Principle #6

Here are actions you can take now to advance LGBT equality. They
are in order of priority; choose those that are more appropriate for
you.

1. DEMAND FULL EQUALITY NOW

When it comes to human rights, there should never be
delays or excuses. We will never get full equality if we do not
even ask for it. Whether you are an insider or an outsider,
demand full equality now from the president (executive
orders, appointments, etc.), Congress, the state legislatures
and governors, and the courts. As Dr. Martin Luther King,
Jr., said, *"A right delayed is a right denied."*

For federal legislation, review the Equality & Religious
Freedom Act (Omnibus Equality Bill) written by Karen
Doering, Esq., and presented by eQualityGiving on March
18, 2009 (www.eQualityGiving.org/Blueprint-for-LGBT-
Equality). We need federal legislation that is comprehensive
and does not negotiate away our equal rights even before it
is introduced. Ask Representative Jared Polis, the senior
openly LGBT member of the House, to introduce
comprehensive legislation instead of a compendium of
existing bills that do not provide full equality.

You can monitor the status of pro-equality federal legislation on www.ActOnPrinciples.org.

Political people will tell you that, as an election year, it is difficult to advance equality in 2014. This is not an excuse for delaying executive action on our equality or take other actions (see the next chapters).

2. HELP IN CRITICAL EQUALITY RACES

Naturally, there is much passion in primary races. However, to advance equality in 2014, the best bang for the buck will be in the general election, especially in selected races. Chapter 55 discusses this strategy as well as the importance of who controls Congress.

3. HELP REACH FULL EQUALITY IN THE STATES

The good news is that we are fully equal under the law in four states (California, Connecticut, New Jersey, Vermont) and the District of Columbia. Contrary to the critics' predictions, the sky has not fallen in states that are pro-equality.

The bad news is that we are unequal in 92 percent of the states. Check here where your state stands: www.eQualityGiving.org/States-of-Equality-and-Gay-Rights-Scorecard

With some hard work, we can soon convert sixteen other states to full equality. Low hanging fruit is in places like Massachusetts, where Democrats control both houses and the governorship. See the details in Chapter 56 and then help. In the other thirty states, it is tougher, but that also means there is more opportunity to have a significant impact; check Chapter 57.

4. HELP WIN BALLOT INITIATIVES

There will likely be ballot initiatives in one or more states to approve marriage equality. It has not been determined yet what states will be ready for such initiatives; among the states being considered for 2014 or 2016 are Oregon, Colorado, Michigan, Ohio, Arkansas, Arizona. They deserve your support because winning in purple states is now in the realm of possibilities. Oregon is expected to bring it in 2014 and, with all of our help, be successful in overturning the constitutional ban on same-gender marriage.

5. HELP WIN IN THE SUPREME COURT (AGAIN)

We need to go back to the Supreme Court to finally win our equal status under the law. Check Chapter 58. This is one area in which efforts can have the greatest impact.

6. PUSH FOR FULL LGBT REPRESENTATION IN THE GOVERNANCE OF OUR ORGANIZATIONS

The boards of directors that govern the LGBT organizations need to fully represent the diversity of our movement. Work with the boards and executive directors of the organizations with which you are involved to ensure full representation. There is particular need of more transgender board members. Thirteen of our largest national LGBT organizations do not have a single transgender board member. Check this transgender board member resource: www.eQualityGiving.org/Transgender-Board-Members

Reread Chapter 32 about what it means to have a movement that is inclusive—and be aware of tokenism, too.

So, ask any organization that you support with your money or time to have a fully representative governing board.

7. DO MAKE IT BETTER FOR OUR YOUTH

After the heart-rending "It Gets Better" campaign by Dan Savage, the issue is how to *make* it better for our youth *now*. This is a topic that needs to be brought up at every town hall meeting for Republicans and Democrats alike.

8. CREATE DIALOG ABOUT RELIGION'S ROLE

Part I of this book prepared you for discussions with family, coworkers, and friends about the freedom of religion. Remember that most religious leaders do not want politicians *to use religion as an excuse for their legislative actions.*

Pope Francis is leading the way towards more acceptance of LGBT people. Follow his lead on this topic.

9. BUILD BRIDGES WITH CORPORATE AMERICA

One of the new challenges after the *Citizens United* decision is that a corporation may give a grant to your favorite LGBT organization while at the same time secretly donate to elect legislators who do not support our equality under the law. We need legislation requiring disclosure of corporate donations. In the meantime, if you are a shareholder activist, you can propose a shareholder vote on disclosure of all the corporate giving.

10. BE A DONOR (SMALL OR LARGE)

If you have never given for equality, consider giving to the organizations mentioned in this book. Or give to fund projects using crowd funding, in which many people give small amounts to projects sponsored by organizations, companies, or individuals—check www.GetGayFunded.com. Support organizations that think bigger and act differently, as well as new organizations and creative individuals with new ideas. Check Chapters 61 and 62 for ideas.

Donors tend to get comfortable with a certain level and way of giving. They should consider being bolder givers and take more risks. A good website to check out is BolderGiving.org. For information on LGBT giving, check eQualityGiving.org, as well as Funders for LGBTQ Issues at LGBTFunders.org.

If you are a donor who has contacts with major foundations, point out to them the five-year $50-million effort by the Ford Foundation to fight for LGBT equality announced in

November 2012.

11. THINK REALLY BIG AND DIFFERENTLY

Don't be limited by mediocrity slogans such as *"Politics is the art of the possible."* Don't stop taking action because it is not possible to pass legislation when the House of Representatives is controlled by the Republican Party. Demand that organizations and elected officials set up specific timetables to reach all the equality goals. Demand full accountability from organizations you donate to: ask for publication of the specific goals they intend to achieve and an annual report of the progress made on achieving those goals.

54.

Make the President Do It

"I agree with you, I want to do it, now make me do
it."

—Franklin D. Roosevelt,
Comment to a group of reformers

President Obama said in 2008 that he would be a fierce advocate for LGBT equality. Four years later he came out for marriage equality, and a year later, in his second inaugural address, he said: *"Our journey is not complete until our gay brothers and sisters are treated like anyone else under the law."*

So, like in the famous quote from President Roosevelt, we have an ally in President Obama, but we need to Make Him Do It.

Most organizations have focused on pushing President Obama to sign a nondiscrimination Executive Order. In reality, thinking bigger, in last year's *Gay Agenda* we pointed out eleven actions that the president could take on his own to expand equality. Here is the status of the actions from last year. Continue pushing to Make Him Do It.

1. NONDISCRIMINATION EXECUTIVE ORDER

The president still needs to sign an executive order protecting federal employees and contractors against discrimination based on sexual orientation and gender identity and expression. Currently, there is Executive Order 13087, signed by President Clinton in 1998, which protects only federal employees (not federal contractors) and only for sexual orientation (this does not include gender identity or expression). There is also Executive Order 11246, signed by President Johnson in 1965, which prohibits federal contractors from discriminating based on race, color, religion, sex, or national origin.

As a presidential candidate in 2008, Barack Obama promised that he would sign such an executive order covering federal employees and contractors (a total of twenty-six million people or about 20 percent of the working population). This promise has not been kept for the last five years.

In March 2012, the president's spokesperson said that the president would not sign such an order until later (implying after the 2012 election). There is no justification for waiting since such an executive order has been drafted and vetted, and it has been ready for President Obama's signature for more than two years.

In April 2012, a poll by the Center for American Progress showed that 69 percent of likely voters in 2012 would support President Obama issuing such an executive order (this includes 83 percent of Democrats, 69 percent of Independents, and 53 percent of Republicans). So more delays and excuses are not acceptable.

This executive order is important because then the performance of the contractors regarding nondiscrimination for sexual orientation and gender identity and expression would be part of the regular reviews performed by the Labor Department's Office of Federal Contract Compliance Programs. The department could then initiate investigations based on employees' complaints or third-party complaints and even on its own since oftentimes employees are reluctant to file a formal complaint. Furthermore, the department could conduct nondiscrimination trainings at the beginning of a federal contract. This is why this executive order is so important in addition to state and federal legislation.

2. MARRIAGE EQUALITY

President Obama needs to be commended in this area as indeed he has been vocal on his support for marriage equality since May 2012. Furthermore, in collaboration with LGBT organizations, his administration has been swift in implementing the 2013 rulings of the Supreme Court, including immediate full equality in benefits for spouses of LGBT service members, full immigration rights, full acceptance by the IRS of same-gender couples even if they live in a discriminatory state.

3. OTHER POLICIES

A group of LGBT organizations published on the web a list of eighty-two federal policy changes listed by agency. They delivered it to the Obama transition team in December 2008. Their most recent update on the web lists sixteen policy changes. This is significant but leaves 80 percent of the changes still pending. Here is a link to their list:
www.thetaskforce.org/newadmin/
newbeginning_scoresheet_5_11.html

Why not insist on a presidential executive order that requires all the government offices under his control to ensure full equal treatment independent of sexual orientation and gender identity within six months? It could include, as minimum requirements, the changes pending and a requirement to establish an ombudsman for equality for each agency (if none exists). It should require a report within six months of the changes made.

4. DON'T ASK DON'T TELL

Under the direction of President Obama, the Secretary of Defense, a Republican, has been strong in implementing equal treatment for all service members. In 2013, nine conservative states refused to provide equal benefits to all married service members in their National Guards; the Secretary of Defense was forceful in requiring all to comply with his directives. All the states complied by the end of the year.

Here are two important items that still need to be completed:

1. Revise the Department of Defense Equal Opportunity Policy to add sexual orientation and gender identity, without it the Department of Defense cannot enforce nondiscrimination.

2. Amend military medical and uniform regulations that discriminate against transgender service members. Allow transgender service members to serve openly.

In addition, there are many issues to be resolved since we only have partial equality or not equality at all in many areas. Read the details about what needs to be done at www.eQualityGiving.org/ DADT which is maintained by Cap. Tom Carpenter, Esq.

5. IMMIGRATION EQUALITY

Thanks to the US Supreme Court ruling in *Windsor,* we have achieved equality in immigration for LGBT people. Applause here the Obama administration which, with the support of LGBT immigration organizations, was very quick in implementing the ruling. For example, in one case a deportation was stopped the same morning that the ruling was issued and, in another case, a gay man obtained his green card two days after the ruling because he was married to an American (the case had been through the administrative process already).

6. TRANSGENDER MEDICAL CARE

The president should also expand the medical care available under Medicare and Medicaid for transgender people. The administration is considering what actions to take on this matter—let's hope for a full resolution in 2014.

7. CABINET MEMBERS

President Obama should appoint an *openly* LGBT cabinet member. This would be an important first in history. Among the many qualified people are Fred Hochberg, currently the president of the Export-Import Bank and previously the head of the Small Business Administration, and Barney Frank, who was chair of the House of Representatives Financial Services Committee.

8. JUDICIAL APPOINTMENTS

When President Obama took office, there was only one openly LGBT federal judge, now there are seven. This is a great improvement, but, as reported by ThinkProgress.org, they constitute only half of one percent of all federal judges.

9. OTHER APPOINTMENTS

President Obama appointed five gay men as ambassadors in 2013. This is a first. He needs to appoint also lesbian, bisexual, and transgender individuals to such positions.

The president appointed Chai Feldblum for another term to the Equal Employment Opportunity Commission, which ruled in 2012 that transgender people are protected against employment discrimination under Title VII of the Civil Rights Act.

10. ORGANIZING FOR ACTION

The president has indicated that he will use his campaign group, Organizing for Action (formerly Organizing for America), and its mailing list, to rally Americans in grassroots efforts to pass his legislative agenda.

He should use this list to help pass legislation for LGBT equality. After all, lesbian, gay, bisexual, and transgender people were significant contributors to and volunteers for his campaign.

11. FIERCE ADVOCATE

President Obama promised six years ago to be a fierce advocate for the LGBT community. Of the eleven actions outlined here last year, he has accomplished two in full, and is half done on six others, while three are still pending (the Executive Order, Cabinet appointments, and Organizing for Action).

Since the president's overall agenda is being stopped by Republicans in the House and Senate, one of his best opportunities for his legacy is to become the president who brought full equality to LGBT Americans. To achieve this depends heavily on the US Supreme Court and Congress, but he can play a very important role by doing all that is possible from an executive perspective. There is still much to do, as the list above shows.

55.

Critical Equality Races

As discussed in Chapter 39, there has been a significant change in the political environment since the Democratic Party adopted a fully pro-equality platform in 2012. This requires a change in strategy for endorsing candidates. The focus now should be on Critical Equality Races. The criteria developed by eQualityGiving for such races are: (1) one candidate is fully pro-equality while the other is anti-equality, (2) the race is close, and (3) funding can make a difference.

Is it better to fund individual candidates or a party? One argument is that if the Democrats had full control of Congress, they could pass equality legislation. There is a hope that they would do so. However, after much lobbying, they only passed two pieces of LGBT equality legislation, one of them incomplete, when they had full control after the 2008 election.

If you fully support the other policies of the Democratic Party, such as healthcare for profit, collecting private data on Americans, drone attacks, etc., then funding the party directly is a good strategy for you. For that, a good vehicle is the Democratic National Committee. If, however, you do not agree with such policies, then it is best to fund Critical Equality Races.

56.

Reaching 100 Percent in the States

We can divide the states into three groups.

The first is the four states (California, Connecticut, New Jersey and Vermont) and the District of Columbia that provide full equality to their LGBT residents according to eQualityGiving's scorecard.

The second group is the sixteen states that, with a laser focus on full equality, could reach it in 2014 and join the first group.

The third consists of the thirty other states lagging significantly behind on equality.

This chapter addresses the second group, and the next chapter discusses the third group.

This is the time for a big push in the states that could get to 100-percent equality this year. The question to ask each state is: what statutes are missing for equal treatment? It is not a matter of just pushing for a specific statute but to push for passage of all statutes needed to bring the state to 100-percent equality.

Here is what needs to be done in these eighteen states and DC (listed by rating and alphabetical within the same rating):

ILLINOIS (92%—up from 83% in 2013)

Illinois changed from civil unions to full marriage equality in 2013, which raised its rating. To get to full equality, Illinois needs to modify the state's hate-crime bill to cover gender identity and expression (it already covers sexual orientation).

IOWA (92%—unchanged since 2012)

This is one of the pioneering states for equality in our country—not just for LGBT rights. In 2012, Democrats maintained their majority in the state Senate, and a state Supreme Court justice who voted for marriage equality was retained despite a fierce campaign against him; both actions suggest that marriage equality is safe for the moment in Iowa.

To reach full LGBT legal equality, Iowa is only missing a statute to handle parenting rights (adoption) for LGBT people. However, with a Republican governor and assembly, to go the last mile will require some work.

COLORADO (83%—unchanged since 2012)

In 2013, Colorado updated the domestic partnerships statute to civil union. An important, but modest step (not enough to change the rating).

Colorado should also address any inequalities for transgender people (especially related to amended birth certificates). These changes would bring the state from a current rating of 83 percent to 92 percent.

To go the final mile to full equality would require rescinding the state's constitutional amendment against same-gender marriage.

MASSACHUSETTS (83%—unchanged since 2012)

Massachusetts could easily provide 100-percent legal equality to its LGBT residents by accomplishing two simple tasks for a legislature with a supermajority of Democrats and a governor who is a big supporter of equality:

1. Add protection in public accommodations for gender identity and expression to its nondiscrimination statute.

2. Add gender identity and expression to its anti-bullying statute.

MINNESOTA (83%—up from 67% in 2013)

After passing marriage equality in 2013, Minnesota needs to complete two items to reach full LGBT equality:

1. Change birth certificates for transgender people as a matter of statute as opposed to the current system, which depends on the courts.

2. Ensure, by statute, that LGBT people can become parents by allowing these three types of adoption: single, joint, and second-parent.

NEW YORK (83%—unchanged since 2012)

After the bipartisan victory for marriage equality in the state in 2011, New York rates at 83 percent and can reach 100 percent if it achieves a couple of long-sought goals:

1. Add gender identity and expression to the existing nondiscrimination statutes regarding employment, housing, credit, and public accommodations.

2. Add gender identity and expression to the state's hate-crime statute, which already covers sexual orientation.

WASHINGTON (83%—unchanged since 2012)

Emboldened by the victory of the popular vote supporting marriage equality in 2012, and with a very supporting governor, state house, and state senate, Washington could pass in short order the statutes to provide full legal equality to its LGBT residents:

1. Equal treatment of birth certificates for transgender people. Currently, this is done by policy; it should be by statute.

2. Ensure that the three types of adoption (single, joint, and second-parent) are available to LGBT people who want to be parents. Currently, this is a common practice but it is not done by statute.

Washington is an example of a state that is already doing the right things; it just needs to codify them in statutes.

DELAWARE (75%—up from 50% in 2013)

Big changes in Delaware in 2013 by changing civil unions to full marriage and adding gender identity and expression to the hate crimes and nondiscrimination status. This is a state with a Democratic governor and Democratic state house and senate. Only two more items to be accomplished for full LGBT equality:

1. Create an anti-bullying statute covering sexual orientation and gender identity and expression.

2. Ensure, by statute, that LGBT people can become parents by allowing these three types of adoption: single, joint, and second-parent.

HAWAII (75%—up from 67% in 2013)

With a governor, house, and senate all fully Democratic, this state should do a big push to complete LGBT equality, after historically passing marriage equality in 2013. Two items are missing:

1. Pass anti-bullying legislation that covers sexual orientation and gender identity and expression.

2. Ensure, by statute, that LGBT people can become parents by allowing these three types of adoption: single, joint, and second-parent.

MAINE (75%—unchanged since 2012)

After the tremendous victory in the popular vote for marriage equality in November 2012, Maine has used the momentum to complete the task for full equality. Only three key items are missing:

1. Add gender identity and expression to the hate-crime statute that already covers sexual orientation.

2. Treat transgender people equally (especially missing is the treatment of birth certificates).

3. Add second-parent adoption.

With a state House and Senate controlled by the Democrats, it should be possible to pass this legislation. Note, however, that the governor is a Republican.

MARYLAND (75%—unchanged since 2012)

Like Maine, this state passed marriage equality by popular vote in 2012 and has a similar gap to achieve full LGBT legal equality. However, Maryland has the advantage of having a governor eager to please in search of a national spotlight to run for president and a House of Delegates and senate with an overwhelming majority of Democrats. Here is what needs to be done:

1. Add gender identity and expression to nondiscrimination statutes for employment, housing, credit, and public accommodations.

2. Treat transgender people equally (especially missing is the treatment of birth certificates).

3. Ensure, by statute, that LGBT people can become parents by allowing these three types of adoption: single, joint, and second-parent.

NEW MEXICO (75%—up from 67% in 2013)

The New Mexico Supreme Court ruled in December 2013 in favor of marriage equality. This is a state with Democratic majorities in the state house and senate, but with a Republican governor. Here is what is missing for full LGBT legal equality:

1. Anti-bullying legislation specifying sexual orientation and gender identity and expression.

2. Ensure, by statute, that LGBT people can become parents by allowing these three types of adoption: single, joint, and second-parent.

OREGON (75%—unchanged since 2012)

With a shift in the legislature in the 2012 election, Oregon now has a Democratic governor and Democratic control of the state house and senate. In addition, the new speaker of the state House, Tina Kotek, is openly lesbian. This is what needs to be done:

1. Pass marriage equality by reversing the constitutional amendment, this is likely to happen by popular vote in 2014.

2. Change birth certificates for transgender people to indicate the correct gender.

3. Ensure, by statute, that LGBT people can become parents by allowing these three types of adoption: single, joint, and second-parent.

NEVADA (67%—up from 50% in 2013)

Here is an example of a Republican governor signing pro-equality legislation in 2013 adding gender identity to the state hate crimes statute (which already covered sexual orientation). Still it will require some work to bring Nevada to 100 percent given that it has a Republican governor, a Democratic assembly, and a senate with a slim Democratic majority (eleven to ten). Here is what needs to be done:

1. Provide marriage equality (the state already has domestic partnerships), but need to overturn the constitutional amendment banning same-gender marriage.

2. Create an anti-bullying statute covering sexual orientation and gender identity and expression.

3. Ensure, by statute, that LGBT people can become parents by allowing these three types of adoption: single, joint, and second-parent.

NEW HAMPSHIRE (67%—unchanged since 2012)

With a new Democratic governor, a state house of representatives with an ample Democratic majority, and a state senate with a slight thirteen-to-eleven Republican majority, New Hampshire can finish the job of providing full LGBT equality. The heavy lifting has already been done by passing civil unions and later same-gender marriage. This is what is missing:

1. Add gender identity and expression to the hate-crime statute that already includes sexual orientation.

2. Add gender identity and expression to the statutes for non discrimination in employment, housing, credit, and public accommodations (which already include sexual orientation).

3. Ensure that birth certificates indicate the correct gender for transgender people.

4. Ensure, by statute, that LGBT people can become parents by allowing these three types of adoption: single, joint, and second-parent.

RHODE ISLAND (58%—up from 50% in 2013)

Rhode Island has an overwhelming Democratic majority in the state senate and house (with a gay speaker of the house, Gordon Fox) and a governor, Lincoln Chafee, who is an independent and who is totally pro-equality. After passing marriage equality in 2013, here is what needs to be done for full equality:

1. Add gender identity and expression to the hate-crime statute (which already covers sexual orientation).

2. Ensure that birth certificates indicate the correct gender for transgender people.

3. Create an anti-bullying statute covering sexual orientation and gender identity and expression.

4. Ensure, by statute, that LGBT people can become parents by allowing these three types of adoption: single, joint, and second-parent.

In 2013, two states (California and New Jersey) and the District of Columbia reached full equality. How many of the sixteen states listed above will reach full LGBT equality in 2014? The time is now for a big push.

What about the other thirty states? Read on.

57.

The Other Thirty States

While four states and the District of Columbia have achieved full LGBT equality and sixteen others could achieve it with a focused push, in the other thirty states, it is more challenging. In most of these thirty states, the conservatives control the governorships and the legislatures. Progress can indeed be made, but it does require creative thinking and new approaches to break through. In the short term, most relief will come from passing federal legislation and through the rulings of the courts. All of these states, except for Indiana, Pennsylvania, West Virginia, and Wyoming, have constitutional amendments defining marriage as between one man and one woman, which will have to be overturned by the courts or popular vote.

These thirty states are: Alabama, Alaska, Arizona, Arkansas, Florida, Georgia, Idaho, Indiana, Kansas, Kentucky, Louisiana, Michigan, Mississippi, Missouri, Montana, Nebraska, North Carolina, North Dakota, Ohio, Oklahoma, Pennsylvania, South Carolina, South Dakota, Tennessee, Texas, Utah, Virginia, West Virginia, Wisconsin, and Wyoming.

Here is the status of each equality goal in these states, as a group.

EQUALITY GOAL: NONDISCRIMINATION

This has been an elusive goal to achieve, despite its having been supported for long time by a large majority of Americans and being fundamental for every person's well-being. Without nondiscrimination protections, most people are not able to be out of the closet and be true to who they are or able to contribute to society up to their potential.

Another reality is that, in some more progressive states, the state statutes are stronger than the federal ones. However, conservative states that currently do not have nondiscrimination statutes for sexual orientation and gender identity are not expected to create stronger ones than the proposed federal law.

Of the thirty states in this group, twenty-nine do not offer any nondiscrimination protection for LGBT people. Only one state (Wisconsin) offers protection, but limited to sexual orientation.

Progress can still happen. For instance, the Republican Governor of Pennsylvania supports a law that would add sexual orientation and gender identity to the nondiscrimination statute.

Fortunately, transgender people are now protected nationwide against employment discrimination under Title VII of the Civil Rights Act.

EQUALITY GOAL: MARRIAGE EQUALITY

The results here are abysmal: except for Wisconsin, which offers domestic partnerships, none of the other twenty-nine states offers any type of statewide recognition of same-gender relationships.

However, with 46 lawsuits going on in 22 states (and more being added), significant progress can occur. For instance, on December 20, 2013, Robert Shelby, a federal district court judge, ruled that Utah's prohibition of same-gender marriage was unconstitutional. Same gender couples started marrying that evening. This is a decision that will be certainly appealed. Interestingly enough, Judge Shelby was appointed by President Obama with the recommendation of Republican US senator Orrin Hatch, who represents Utah.

EQUALITY GOAL: PROTECTING YOUTH

Of the thirty states in this group, only North Carolina and West Virginia offer critical anti-bullying legislation with specific enumeration of sexual orientation and gender identity and expression. Wisconsin offers protection based only on sexual orientation. The other states offer nothing.

Research conducted by GLSEN shows that anti-bullying statutes must identify specific groups protected by the legislation, otherwise it is not effective, so we do not count states with generic policies (such as Florida).

EQUALITY GOAL: PARENTING

Parenting and adoption is mostly a state issue and, in most cases, is handled through the courts on a case-by-case basis rather than by statute. Of these states, Indiana is the only one offering the three types of adoption needed for legal equality: (1) a single LGBT person adopting, (2) joint adoption by a same-gender couple, and (3) second-parent adoption by a same-gender couple.

Beyond Indiana, adoption in the other states depends on the jurisdiction within the state, or it has not been tested.

EQUALITY GOAL: FREEDOM OF GENDER

There is a multitude of approaches in these thirty states regarding birth certificates:

- In one state (Indiana), there is no indication of gender in the birth certificate.

- In ten states, a new birth certificate is issued with the new gender.

- In three states (Idaho, Ohio, and Tennessee), the original gender in the birth certificate cannot be changed.

- In three states (Montana, Texas, and Wisconsin), a court or court clerk makes the decision.

- In the rest of the states, the birth certificate is amended (still showing the gender at birth).

The model bill regarding changes in birth certificates is the JaParker Deoni Jones Birth Certificate Amendment Act, approved unanimously by the District of Columbia Council in 2013.

EQUALITY GOAL: HATE CRIMES

Since 2009, there has been federal hate crimes legislation which covers sexual orientation and gender identity. This legislation is very useful, but it is not a replacement for hate-crime legislation in the states.

Of the thirty states in our group, only one (Missouri) offers a hate-crime statute covering sexual orientation and gender identity and expression. Nine others offer protection only for sexual orientation. The other twenty offer no protection. There is still a long way to go in many states.

58.

Back to the Supremes

"Equal Justice Under Law"

—Inscription in façade of Supreme Court Building

Marriage equality is becoming increasingly prevalent with seventeen states and the District of Columbia now granting civil marriage licenses without gender discrimination (in addition, Utah is under appeal).

This piecemeal, state-by-state approach posses a practical problem: say that you are married and live in a state that allows same-gender marriages, what happens when you travel or move to another state that does not recognize your marriage? It is a practical nightmare if states do not recognize your marriage.

Currently there are forty-six legal cases in twenty-two states addressing marriage equality and other LGBT issues, and more are being added. The floodgates are wide open and without any doubt, in less than three years, the US Supreme Court will be asked to rule again on marriage.

One issue to be addressed by the Court is whether other states should recognize the marriage from another state. One could claim that states have the right to chose who can get married. In practice, what is at stake is whether we are one country, in which we can travel and relocate freely while the most important commitment between two people maintains recognition.

A second issue is whether all states and territories should allow same-gender couples to get married. This corresponds to whether marriage is considered a fundamental right (as the Supreme Court has proclaimed on multiple occasions). As such, same-gender couples should be able to marry in each state and territory.

The central issue is what prevails: the states' rights to regulate marriage or the individuals' rights to liberty and equal protection under the law? In his ruling stating that Utah's prohibition of same-gender marriages was unconstitutional, district court judge Robert Shelby wrote:

> The [US Supreme] Court has held that the Fourteenth Amendment requires that individual rights take precedence over states' rights where these two interests are in conflict.

In 1967, some states allowed interracial marriages and some did not. At that time, the vast majority of the country's population opposed interracial marriage (while in 2013, the majority supported same-gender marriage). Back then in some states, legally married interracial couples could be put in jail. The Supreme Court in the famous 1967 *Loving v. Virginia* case made interracial marriages valid in all states and territories. This was the most fair and practical solution to a patchwork of states with vastly different requirements for marriage. More importantly, this upheld the Constitution's belief in the supremacy of individual rights and the equal treatment of all individuals under the law.

To show the dignity of our relationships and the importance that our marriages are valid everywhere, this author started the internet campaign www.LovingEverywhere.com. It is a call to action to send a picture of you as a couple to each member of the Supreme Court (whether you are a same-gender or different-gender couple) and other courts and legislators in your state showing your humanity and dignity and the obvious need for Loving Everywhere.

To bring cases to the US Supreme Court is a very lengthy process that requires significant resources. Since we do not know which cases will end up there, it is worth supporting all the LGBT legal organizations which are doing a great job. This work is nowadays the best bang for the donors' buck. These organizations are:

- ACLU Lesbian and Gay Rights Project (ACLU.org/LGBT-rights)

- American Foundation for Equal Rights (AFER.org)

- Gay and Lesbian Defenders & Advocates (GLAD.org)

- Lambda Legal (LambdaLegal.org)

- National Center for Lesbian Rights (NCLRights.org)

The next two chapters address techniques for being a strategic donor.

59.

How Much Is Equality Worth to *You?*

Equality doesn't just happen on its own. Many people give substantial amounts of money, time, and talent to make it happen.

The culture of giving is important, regardless of how much money you have. Consider any of the ideas below (or create your own) depending on your financial situation:

1. *Give a few dollars.*
   Most people can donate a few dollars from time to time. No matter how much you can afford, giving helps bring equality.

2. *Give some percentage of your annual income.*
   This is a common formula—for example, give 10 percent of your annual income, as some religious traditions suggest (tithing toward a worthy cause).

3. *Give some percentage of your net assets (or your assets in stock investments).*
   Many experts believe that if you spend less than 4 percent per year of your invested assets, you will not run out of money in your lifetime, and your assets will still keep up with inflation. Of course, this is based on many assumptions, so you need to check with your financial advisor.

4. *Give some percentage of your disposable income.*
   Deduct from your income your basic expenses: taxes, mortgage, and basic living expenses. Then give some percentage of what's left to advance equality.

5. *Give a part of your annual bonus.*
   In their minds, people do not count bonuses as part of regular income. So why not use part of it to obtain your legal rights (for example, to ensure that you or cannot be fired solely for your sexual orientation of gender identity)?

A SIMPLE GIVING PLAN

There are many causes that deserve your money, but if you or someone you love is lesbian, gay, bisexual, or transgender, why not give first to promote fundamental fairness?

It is easy to create a giving plan. Start by considering three main buckets in which to put your money:

1. Amount you want to give in the next twelve months to advance LGBT equality: $_____

2. Amount you want to give in the next twelve months to other LGBT issues (e.g., HIV, Arts): $_____

3. Amount you want to give in the next twelve months to non-LGBT issues: $_____

For the amount that you want to give to advance equality (first bucket), consider the following split:

• 40 percent for politicians and political organizations that will assist in passing legislation for equality (in election years, maybe this should be 60 percent);

• 40 percent for nonprofits working to achieve equality (in election years, maybe this should be 30 percent);

• 10 percent for opportunity giving (in election years, maybe this is reduced to 5 percent); and

• 10 percent for social-obligations giving (in election years, maybe reduce to 5 percent)

These percentages are just a guideline. Modify them to suit your interests, but it is important to stick to an allocation that makes sense for you and your interests.

A culture of giving will do wonders for your spirit and, combined with the donations of other people, will lead to change.

If you have the financial means, the next chapter is for you— otherwise, just skip it.

60.

Strategic and Creative Donors

Advances in equality have occurred because of the dedication and sacrifices of many grassroots volunteers, elected officials, and staff people working for nonprofits and many people fortunate enough (and generous enough) to fund the movement.

This chapter focuses on big donors. It discusses fourteen different strategies they can follow for their giving. There are many terms used to describe strategic philanthropy: intelligent giving, strategic giving, effective philanthropy, venture philanthropy, inspired philanthropy.

Donors, especially mega donors, can create a unique combination of strategies that best fit their needs—for more details on these strategies, including online resources, please check: www.eQualityGiving.org/Giving-Center.

1. IMPACT GIVING

Donors concentrate their giving on a few organizations, political candidates, or equality goals with *large* donations that have a significant impact.

Good for:

- Donors with large budgets
- Donors with solid strategic visions that can change the movement

2. ORGANIZATIONAL GIVING

Donors concentrate most of their giving on a single organization.

Good for:

- Members of the board of that organization, as well as its senior employees
- Donors whose professional interests match the organization direction (e.g., an attorney giving to a legal defense organization)

3. GOAL GIVING

Donors concentrate their giving on achieving an equality goal instead of on an organization.

Good for:

- Donors passionate to achieve specific equality goals (e.g., protecting youth or marriage equality)

4. CONCENTRATED GIVING

Donors give to a limited number of organizations and political candidates.

Good for:

- Donors with more limited budgets
- Donors who are very strategic

5. DISPERSED GIVING

In this strategy, donors give to a multitude of organizations and political candidates.

Good for:

- Donors with large budgets
- Donors who have a hard time saying no
- Donors who fundraise for other causes—this approach creates goodwill among donors who support each other's causes.

6. OPPORTUNITY GIVING

Donors give to take advantage of an immediate opportunity that will achieve a tangible result in a short time (usually a year or less).

Good for:

- Donors who want to see immediate results

7. CAPACITY GIVING

Donors give to build the capacity of an organization or political party and make them more robust over a long time.

Good for:

- Donors who know and trust the senior leadership of the organization and believe in the potential of its mission

8. LOCAL GIVING

Donors give to organizations and politicians in their local communities and states.

Good for:

- Donors who want to make a tangible difference in the lives of their communities
- Donors who want to get to know and influence their local and state politicians

9. MAVERICK GIVING

Donors who want to give to unconventional causes or lesser-known organizations/politicians.

Good for:

- Donors who like to create new paths

10. ANGEL GIVING

Donors who give to help new organizations get established.

Good for:

- Donors interested in social entrepreneurship

11. GAP GIVING

Donors review each of the equality goals and each of the strategic approaches to achieve LGBT equality and give to the areas that are insufficiently funded.

Good for:

- Donors with considerable financial means
- Donors interested in strategic analysis

12. COLLABORATIVE GIVING

Donors give jointly with other donors in the pursuit of a common goal. Examples of this approach are giving circles and some foundations. There are two flavors to collaborative giving: (1) donors give to a fund and a committee distributes the money; or (2) donors are presented with a set of options, and they decide individually how much to give to each of the options.

Good for:

- Donors sharing common passions
- Donors who do not have the time or interest in researching the potential grantees by themselves

13. CONVEYOR GIVING

Donors decide on a goal to be achieved and search for the proper organizations or groups to help achieve it jointly. Donors, in effect, convey a group of organizations and people for a joint goal.

Good for:

- Donors with significant giving capabilities
- Donors respected by the groups that they are conveying
- Donors with the time and abilities to bring together different groups

14. SOCIAL GIVING

Donors give based on social obligations and requests from friends.

Good for:

- Donors who do not want to say no

If you are a big donor, you can use one or more of the strategies presented to maximize the impact of your giving, taking into account your personal situation.

61.

Acting Differently

"Here's to the crazy ones, the misfits, the rebels, the
troublemakers, the round pegs in the square holes...
because the people who are crazy enough to think
that they can change the world are the ones that
do."

—Original text for the first "Think different"
Apple commercial, 1997
Narrated by Steve Jobs

An important way to accelerate reaching equality is by *acting differently*: pushing the envelope and creating new ideas and approaches because many times progress comes from unexpected sources. Below are some stories that highlight acting differently. Use them just as pointers. Do not let anyone discourage you from taking action, because nobody really knows which actions will stick and resonate with the public. Go for it!

GOING TO THE SUPREME COURT

The legal organizations working for LGBT equality have done an outstanding job securing more and more victories in the courts, including the critical 2003 victory of *Lawrence v. Texas* in the Supreme Court, which decriminalized homosexuality.

Regarding the right to marry, the LGBT legal organizations have been building the case very carefully and wanted all their ducks in a row before going to the US Supreme Court. All of this changed in 2009 when Chad Griffin, a non-lawyer with significant contacts in Hollywood, asked himself, *Why not bring a marriage case to the Supreme Court now?* Of course, very aware of the risks, he then said, *What if we go to the Supreme Court with a dream team of lawyers?*

There are a couple of attorneys who come up when seeking representation in front of the Supreme Court: Ted Olson, a conservative, who represented George W. Bush in *Bush v. Gore*, the lawsuit in 2000 that decided the campaign for the most important job on the planet; and David Boies, a liberal with extensive Supreme Court experience, who represented Al Gore in the same case. What if you could have a conservative and a liberal, Olson and Boies, both on the same side in front of the Supreme Court, presenting the case for marriage equality? This would be a dream come true! Well, Chad Griffin made it happen (although his approach was considered controversial and risky by many heads of equality organizations). Chad founded the American Foundation for Equal Rights (afer.org) in 2009 and was very successful in raising the funds needed for this lawsuit. Now Chad is the president of the Human Rights Campaign, the largest LGBT political organization.

The Olson-Boies team won marriage equality in California. They are now working to bring another case to the US Supreme Court to bring marriage equality in all states and territories.

GOING BY FOOT

On June 9, 2012, activist Richard Noble completed the first solo walk for LGBT equality across the country, carrying the LGBT flag, and obtaining many proclamations along the way in support of the American Equality Bill—a single, comprehensive bill for LGBT legal equality.

Richard's 2,700-mile walk took fifteen months to complete. Even without receiving much support from most LGBT organizations, the walk achieved its goal of raising awareness for the need for legal equality and doing it now with a single bill.

GOING TO THE STREETS

November 4, 2008, was a sad day for equal rights: a referendum in California took away the right to marry in that state for same-gender couples. Just two weeks after that vote, there were demonstrations all around the country in support of marriage equality. Who organized these demonstrations? The largest LGBT organizations? No. They were organized by just two people out of

Seattle with a computer and much passion and creativity—an example of acting differently and boldly. Now the right for same-gender couples to marry in California has been restored by the US Supreme Court.

GOING WILD

A new organization, GetEqual, the brainchild of Paul Yandura and Jonathan Lewis, created quite a bit of good havoc by using civil disobedience techniques. Founded in 2010, it represents the spirit of the Dallas Principles:
Full Equality Now. No Delays. No Excuses.

GetEqual, with its direct actions, such as its members chaining themselves to the fence of the White House, is a key organization to raise awareness that we need equality now.

GOING TO THE WHITE HOUSE

President Obama had promised to repeal "Don't Ask, Don't Tell." Many actions helped to make it happen: the lawsuit won by Log Cabin Republicans, SLDN's lobbying Congress, donors' pushing key senators behind the scenes, a new organization (OutServe) of underground LGBT service members, and many other actions.

An action that was very different was Dan Choi and several others chaining themselves to the White House fence. It had a significant impact on the news and highlighted very publicly the need to repeal "Don't Ask, Don't Tell."

What should have been a small case of civil disobedience became a bigger issue as they got arrested and some of them faced trial (which they won after two years of legal battles).

GOING TO WORK

For forty years, we have tried to pass federal legislation to protect against employment discrimination. There have been no results as of yet. So Tico Almeida, an employment attorney who worked as lead counsel in the US House of Representatives on the proposal to ban workplace discrimination against LGBT people, decided to start Freedom to Work in the fall of 2011. This is a good example of an organization focusing on a single equality goal to get the job done.

GOING TO CHURCH

There are multiple organizations that take the soft approach to work with different religious faiths to make them more accepting of homosexuality. Taking a different approach, Mitchell Gold founded FaithInAmerica.org in December 2005 to directly confront the harm caused by religious bigotry. This is yet another example of a creative individual (he is the cofounder of Gold +Williams furniture design and manufacturing) acting differently. Mitchell Gold wrote an important book about LGBT, *Crisis: 40 Stories Revealing the Personal, Social, and Religious Pain and Trauma of Growing Up Gay in America*.

GOING TO GRADUATE SCHOOL

Chuck Williams noticed an important gap in our tools to achieve LGBT legal equality: the need for rigorous, independent research and scholarship on issues of LGBT law and public policy. So he started the Williams Institute (WilliamsInstitute.law.ucla.edu) in 2001 and hosted it at the UCLA School of Law to demonstrate the seriousness and quality of the research. The Williams Institute has done pioneering research on the census and LGBT demographics, economic impact of marriage equality, parenting, safe schools, and much more.

GOING AFTER THEM

There are several good examples of individuals going after closeted politicians who voted against equality.

For many years, through his www.BlogActive.com website, Mike Rogers reported about politicians that were in the closet while voting against equality. He was instrumental in having several of them to vote in favor of equality.

In 2006, Mark Foley resigned from Congress after Lane Hudson publicized his sexually explicit text messages and emails. This led to an outcry, and many observers credit this case with helping the Democrats to gain back the House of Representatives.

In 2009, Kirby Dick released *Outrage*, a documentary about politicians who are in the closet and vote against equality.

GOING YOUR WAY

The stories above illustrate the importance of creativity and acting differently.

Whether you are a volunteer, a donor, an activist, an ally, the head of an organization, or a bystander, by acting differently, you can achieve what old methods have not. Dream it...and take action.

62.

Your Turn: Supporting Organizations

This chapter is for people who are (or want to become) donors to organizations for equality. Before you think about supporting an organization, think about which equality goal you are most passionate about. Is it marriage? Is it employment nondiscrimination? Is it freedom of gender? Or another one? Then reread the chapter of this book in Part II that discusses that goal. You will see mentioned there good organizations whose missions are aligned with that goal. Of course, there might be other good organizations (especially at the state level) that may not be mentioned in this book.

Another approach is to focus on the paths to reach equality instead of a specific equality goal. These paths are discussed in Part III of this book. Focusing on a path is very appropriate if you have a specialty that matches it. For instance, if you are an attorney, your focus may not be on a single goal but to reach equality through the courts.

If your focus is religion, check organizations focused on this, such as the InterfaithAlliance.org and the ReligiousInstitute.org. For a different perspective on religion, check FaithInAmerica.org.

When giving to nonprofit organizations, consider these tips:

- *Give for multiple years*
  Some people recommend three-year commitments, but your commitment should be until a specific goal is reached.

- *Give consistently*
  In election years, it is very tempting to give more for political issues at the expense of the nonprofits. Organizations need stability, so continue supporting them despite the notion that this might be the "election of a lifetime."

- *Check outcomes, not just general progress in the movement*
  What has the organization achieved specifically each year for equality? How relevant is this to achieving legal equality? Does the organization have a written plan with the specific goals to be achieved that year?

- *Help with unplanned opportunities*
  In a perfect world, organizations would know what they are going to do for the whole year. In reality, new funding may be required to take advantage of a new opportunity. For example, an organization may need extra money to fund a survey on a new development. This is not an excuse for organizations that not plan properly. It is helpful to be there for well-managed organizations that want to make the best of a new situation.

- *Ask for goal-based accountability*
  Annual reports that are not based on pre-established goals are of limited value to the board, donors, and volunteers. Ask the organization to announce its goals for the short term and long term and report at least annually on the progress towards those goals. The organization needs to establish clearly what it expects to be its contribution to achieve each specific goal.

- *Ask more*
  The organizations that you support should think big and act differently. They should have a governing board that is fully inclusive of our community, including transgender people.

For the next chapter, let's turn our attention to specific actions you can take to support equality in 2013.

63.

Your Turn, Your Way

So many equality goals, so many paths to reach equality, so many priorities, so many actions you can take. How do you choose?

Choose your goal based on your *passion*.

Choose your path based on your *skills*.

If you have the passion, the skills, and the proper resources for the task (money or time), you can push for equality your own way—without following the established paths.

For example, in September 2010, Dan Savage created, basically single-handedly, the important campaign "It Gets Better." Within two months, President Obama and many others in his administration had produced a video to tell LGBT youth that it gets better.

Here's one more example: a donor friend saw a need in his town to help LGBT high school seniors have their own prom so they could be themselves. He made it happen for fifteen hundred dollars. It has been among the most satisfying cases of giving in his (generous) life as a philanthropist.

Here's a final example: another friend studied the new restrictive registration laws in Florida and determined ways to comply with them at a minimum cost so that the maximum number of people could be registered. His efforts made a difference in 2012 in this critical battleground state.

So, how do you go about going your own way?

Consider these four approaches:

1. *The Highway*
   In this approach, you go through an established organization

(maybe you are on its board or are a volunteer or donor). Here are the steps that you follow:

1. Have an idea
2. Discuss the idea
3. Present the idea to the board
4. Improve the idea based on feedback
5. Get approval for the idea
6. Fundraise to pay for it
7. Do it!

2. *The Shortcut*
   Here, you just do it yourself—no bureaucracies.
   1. Have an idea
   2. Do it!

   This works very well if you are a very creative person and just use standard (and free) tools such as Facebook, Twitter, YouTube, blogs, and others.

3. *The Expert's Way*
   In this case, you become an expert (for example, in strategic giving) and help make a big step forward for equality. This method requires talent and much patience since it is very time-consuming. But it is priceless.

4. *No Road*
   In the ultimate freedom, you decide not to follow any of the paths above. Just do some constant random acts that move us closer to equality. Be creative. The dots will connect one day.

If you can go on your own path and are very creative, you can have a very significant impact. Remember Apple's commercial quoted at the beginning of Part IV of this book:

> "Here's to the crazy ones, the misfits, the rebels, the troublemakers, the round pegs in the square holes... because the people who are crazy enough to think that they can change the world are the ones that do."

Is this you? It certainly is *me*. The next chapter presents my own path.

64.

My Turn, My Way

"A two-man activist factory."

—Jesse Monteagudo

In a review of the 2013 edition of the *Gay Agenda*, Jesse Monteagudo coined the phrase "A two-man activist factory" in referring to the work of my spouse and I. Allow me in this chapter to adopt the first person to describe the path I chose. This book is not about theories about equality, it is all based on things I have done myself.

The path I chose for equality was very simple. First, identify what the goals are (I created the term equality goals). Second, determine the steps required to achieve those goals. Third, create the tools to make this a reality.

In summary, gaining equality under the law is all about creating the intellectual framework of what needs to be done and then creating the tools to do it. In reality, I am a tool creator. These tools help accelerate reaching equality.

So here is what this is all about in more detail:

1. **IMMEDIATE GOAL: EQUAL UNDER THE LAW**

   We should not confuse legal equality with social justice or equality in real terms. The immediate and necessary goal is to reach equality under the law.

   TOOL CREATED: Equality Goals
   By comparing the protections of what other groups have and the LGBT people do not have, it is easy to set the equality goals—the protections under the law that we are missing. These goals are explained in detail in Part II of this book.

TOOL CREATED: eQualityGiving.org website
This website is focused on how donors can accelerate achieving LGBT legal equality. It is organized based on the equality goals. All other major LGBT organizations arrange their websites by issues (which are very different from goals).

2. EQUALITY GOALS IN LEGAL TERMS

Once you have the equality goals, it is important to write them in legal terms so that they can be enacted as legislation.

TOOLS CREATED: Omnibus Equality Bill and American Equality Bill
These tools serve to tell legislators: this is what we want—no more, no less than other groups. This *is* the gay agenda.

These proposed bills also serve as model bills so that, even if legislation is introduced affecting only one part that is covered in the omnibus bill, it serves as a reference in case that bill gets watered down before passage. This legislation was written at my request by Karen M. Doering, Esq., a great lawyer specializing in nondiscrimination law.

The American Equality Bill, championed by J. Todd Fernandez, Esq., is the subset of the omnibus bill that focuses on adding the terms *sexual orientation* and *gender identity* to the Civil Rights Act.

3. STRATEGY TO REACH THE EQUALITY GOALS

Once we have identified the equality goals, it is easy to determine the basic strategy. Which goals are better addressed in states and which ones at the federal level? What's the priority? What's the investment required?

TOOL CREATED: Strategic Matrices
These matrices address the questions above in a clear manner. They are available at www.eQualityGiving.org/Giving-to-Charity-Guide.

TOOL CREATED: Discussion Network

A network of major and mega donors, executive directors of LGBT organizations, pro-equality elected officials and endorsed candidates, and thought leaders who discuss how to achieve LGBT equality.

4. CANDIDATE ENDORSEMENT AND CRITICAL RACES

Because the main objective is to be equal under the law, candidate endorsements are very important—since candidates are the future legislators who will vote for our equality.

TOOLS CREATED: Endorsement Framework and Endorsed Candidates List
The framework and the endorsement criteria are unique: www.eQualityGiving.org/Endorsements.

This framework is used for actual endorsements in which every candidate submits a questionnaire that can be made public and is personally interviewed (with the exception of President Obama, with whom I spoke but not in a formal endorsement interview):
www.eQualityGiving.org/Endorsed-Candidates
From this information the Critical Equality Races are determined.

5. FOLLOW THROUGH

After the elections, it is very important to follow through and ensure that legislation is being introduced, voted on, and passed.

Is a bill ready to be voted on? How many votes do we have? To answer these questions, the leadership of the House and Senate conduct whip counts, in which they poll members of their own parties about their positions on a piece of legislation. Whip counts are also conducted at the state level. Lobbyists conduct their own whip counts (although usually partially, since it is very labor-intensive).

TOOL CREATED: www.ActOnPrinciples.org
This is a unique tool that makes whip counts public and allows a registered user to update the whip count. There is

nothing like it anywhere else. The information is kept up-to-date by Donald Hitchcock.

TOOL CREATED: Platform for Other Contributors
By creating a versatile platform, specific web pages can be created very quickly that allow others to lead important projects. For example:

1. Andrew Tobias, treasurer of the Democratic National Committee, created and keeps updated the most comprehensive list available of accomplishments by the administration and Congress on LGBT equality: www.eQualityGiving.org/Accomplishments-by-the-Administration-and-Congress-on-LGBT-Equality.

2. Ret. Captain Tom Carpenter, Esq., created the list of issues pending after the repeal of "Don't Ask, Don't Tell": www.eQualityGiving.org/DADT.

3. Dr. Dana Beyer leads the project to have more transgender board members so that the governance of our organizations represent the full spectrum of LGBT: www.eQualityGiving.org/Transgender-Board-Members.

6. MEASURE PROGRESS

Once you have clear goals, it is imperative to measure progress.

TOOL CREATED: Federal LGBT Legal Equality Index
It is available here:
www.eQualityGiving.org/Equal-Protection-of-the-Law.

TOOL CREATED: States of Equality Scorecard
This rates every state based on the equality goals; it can be sorted by state, by score, and by goal. It is available here: www.eQualityGiving.org/States-of-Equality-and-Gay-Rights-Scorecard.

7. THINK BIGGER, ACT DIFFERENTLY—URGENCY

We need a constant sense of urgency to achieve the equality goals. Because too many people are suffering, legal equality is needed right now. To do so, the movement needs to think bigger and act differently.

TOOL CREATED: THE DALLAS PRINCIPLES
I convened the meeting of twenty-four leaders who created the Dallas Principles, which is described in detail in Chapter 31 and Appendix 2 of this book and is also available online: www.TheDallasPrinciples.com.

TOOL CREATED: eQualityThinking
This was a unique conference, described here: www.eQualityThinking.org.

TOOL CREATED: Loving Everywhere.
A website that asks people to send their pictures and letters to the Supreme Court justices, explaining the practical need for same-gender marriages to be valid and recognized everywhere: www.LovingEverywhere.com.

8. THIS SERIES OF BOOKS

This should be a useful tool since it is intended to be a comprehensive guide to reach legal equality for the LGBT community. Like any good guidebook is updated annually to include the specific actions to take that year.

The final tool mentioned is this book. It includes all my prior work and expands on it—not only the content, but addressing a wider audience. Achieving legal equality is not only important for LGBT people and their allies but for all persons who—independent of their religion or political affiliation—believe in the equality expressed in the United States Constitution and Declaration of Independence.

65.

Summary: Don't Stop

After the electoral victories in 2012 and the victories in the US Supreme Court in 2013, it is time to remember that the fight needs to continue. While every person chooses when to stop volunteering and donating, this is not the time yet for most of us. There is still work to do to accomplish the equality goals.

In 2014, we need to continue demanding full equality both at the federal and state levels; there is no excuse why a few more states, fully controlled by the Democratic Party, cannot provide full LGBT equality now.

We also need to help win elections. The focus is no longer in the primaries; concentrate your efforts in a few Critical Equality Races.

Also, we should continue supporting the LGBT legal organizations, they are fighting legal cases in 22 states and they provide a cost effective pathway for equality.

Choose your own path to help. You may have time but no cash—then volunteer. You may have cash and no time—then give. Better yet, do both.

Do whatever fits your means, time, personality, passion, and skills. The more you can think bigger and act differently, the better.

This is not the time for delays or excuses. This is not the time for outmoded clichés such as *"politics is the art of the possible."* In reality, *politics is the art of leadership*. This is the time for insiders to publicly push for full equality now. This is the time for the president to be our fiercest public advocate. This is the time for Congress and state legislatures to make true the promise of equality under the law. This is also the time for Republicans to join in the promise of equality written in our Declaration of Independence and our Constitution.

A Respectful Message for *You*

- **To President Obama:** *This is your opportunity as a fierce advocate.*
  There is one simple goal: LGBT people treated equally under the law. No delays. No excuses.

- **To legislators:** *Equality under the law is what makes the United States of America a great country.*
  Every day that you delay enacting equality legislation, you are affecting real people, and you are not complying with your oath of office.

- **To a religious person:** *Protect your freedom of religion.*
  Your freedom of religion is only possible if others have freedom of religion. This means that we cannot write civil laws based on any particular religion.

- **To parents and grandparents:** *You determine what your family's values are.*
  Do you love all your children equally? Do you treat them equally? Do you want others to do the same?

- **To teenagers:** *Bullying is not cool.*
  Bullies are immature, cruel, and insecure. Definitely not cool.

- **To LGBT teenagers:** *We will make it better.*
  Teenage years are always difficult—more difficult because of the immature bullies. Truly, it gets better. And many people are working hard every day to make it better now.

- **To bullies:** *We know your game.*
  You might be an immature and cruel teenage bully, not understanding the harmful effects that bullying has on somebody's life. Or you might be an adult political bully, intentionally misleading people about what family values are, what freedom of religion entails, or what the Constitution really means and, in doing so, harming the lives

of many people. But we Americans now know your game and will stand up to protect our Constitution, our family values, our individualism, our freedom of religion, and our unalienable right to happiness. *Game over.*

Epilogue: The Ultimate Goal

The gay agenda is simple: to fulfill the American promise to treat every individual equally under the law—independently of their sexual orientation (heterosexual, homosexual, or bisexual) or their gender identity or expression. So it affects every person.

Imagine living in a country in which:

- Each of us is respected and has an opportunity to develop to our maximum capacity.

- Each of us can pursue happiness on our own terms.

- A religion's laws—whether from Bahai, Buddhism, Christianity, Hinduism, Islam, Judaism, Mormonism, or others—are not imposed on nonmembers.

- The courts are truly independent.

- Each of us is judged by our actions and not prejudged because of the color of our skin, our gender, our race, our national origin, our disability, our religion, our sexual orientation, or our gender identity or expression.

This country already exists, and it is bound by a great Constitution and inscribed in the façade of the Supreme Court building: Equal Under Law.

What needs to be done is known. Time is of the essence because the current unequal treatment causes real damage to real people. So, let's work for:

Full legal equality now. No delays. No excuses.

As you know from reading this book, full equality under the law is the next step, but what is the ultimate goal?

The ultimate goal is a world without prejudice.

As Mother Theresa said: "If you judge people, you have no time to love them."

The irony is that, on one hand, achieving a world without prejudice is a very difficult goal to reach. On the other hand, it can be reached because each of us has the power to stop prejudging others *right now*.

May we all become inspired and live without prejudice.

Thank *You!*

Countless people engaged daily in achieving equality for the LGBT community have influenced the thoughts expressed in this book and in the eQualityGiving website (where parts of this book appeared first).

These people include the authors of the Dallas Principles; all the members of the Discussion Network of eQualityGiving; the eighty-two panelists and twenty-seven question moderators of eQualityThinking; the webmaster, editors, and champions of Act On Principles; the elected officials eQualityGiving has endorsed over the years; the speakers and participants at OutGiving; and the executive directors and staff of equality organizations who work so hard to achieve equality.

Thanks to Doreen Space, my editor, and to Stephen Herbits, Esq. and Michael Krawitz, Esq., who provided many helpful comments.

For more than anybody else, my appreciation and love is for Dr. Ken Ahonen-Jover. He is my soul mate, best friend, sounding board, and spouse.

About the Author

Juan Ahonen-Jover, Ph.D., is an entrepreneur who did well and is now doing good. He is the creator and cofounder of eQualityGiving, ActOnPrinciples, eQualityThinking, and Loving Everywhere and the convener of the Omnibus Bill and the Dallas Principles—all focused on the fundamental principle that everyone should be treated equally under the law.

Juan was awarded a Fulbright fellowship and was educated at Stanford University in supercomputers and business. He has four advanced degrees and is fluent in four languages. He co-authored a book on computers and is an innovator in election protection.

Juan enjoys speaking engagements from time to time. Contact him at www.GayAgenda2014.com.

APPENDIX 1:

Notable LGBT People

This appendix lists a few lesbian, gay, bisexual, and transgender people (LGBT) who are particularly notable. The list is not comprehensive, by any means. We cannot understand the gay agenda without knowing some of the LGBT figures and their contributions to society.

How do we know that these people are gay, lesbian, bisexual, or transgender? Some cases are easy since the person publicly announced his or her sexual orientation or gender identity. For others, there is plenty of historical evidence. If you want to learn more about their contributions to society or their coming out status, Wikipedia has good write-ups about them.

POLITICS AND GOVERNMENT

- **Elio di Rupo** (1951–). Gay. Prime Minister of Belgium since 2011.

- **Johanna Sigurdardottir** (1942–). Lesbian. Prime Minister of Iceland (2009–2013).

- **Per-Kristina Foss** (1950–). Gay. Prime Minister of Norway for a brief period in 2002,.

- **Guido Westerwelle** (1961–). Gay. Vice Chancellor of Germany (2009–2011). Foreign Minister of Germany since 2009.

- **Bertrand Delanoe** (1950–). Gay. Current Mayor of Paris since 2001.

- **Klaus Wowereit** (1953–). Gay. Current Mayor of Berlin since 2001.

- **Annise Parker** (1956–). Lesbian. Current Mayor of Houston since 2010.

- **Christine Quinn** (1966–). Lesbian. Speaker of New York City Council.

- **Tammy Baldwin** (1962–). Lesbian. US Senator (2013–) .First female elected from Wisconsin to the US Congress, first openly LGBT person elected to the US House of Representatives (1999–2013), and first openly LGBT person elected to the US Senate.

- **Barney Frank** (1940–). Gay. Former member of the US House of Representatives (1981–2013). Chairman, House Financial Services Committee (2007–2011). First member of Congress to marry a same-gender spouse (2012).

- **Jared Polis** (1975–). Gay. Member of the US House of Representatives (2009–).

- **David Cicilline** (1961–). Gay. Member of the US House of Representatives (2011–).

- **Sean Patrick Maloney** (1966–). Gay. Member of the US House of Representatives (2013–).

- **Mark Pocan** (1964–). Gay. Member of the US House of Representatives (2013–).

- **Mark Takano** (1960–). Gay. Member of the US House of Representatives (2013–).

- **Kyrsten Sinema** (1976–). Bisexual. Member of the US House of Representatives (2003–). First out bisexual elected to Congress.

- **Michael Michaud** (1955–). Gay. Member of the US House of Representatives (2013–). Came out as gay in 2013.

- **Gerry Studds** (1937–2011). Gay. First Member of Congress to come out while in office.

- **James McGreevey** (1957–). Gay. Governor of New Jersey (2002–2004).

- **Kate Brown** (1960–). Bisexual. Oregon Secretary of State (2009–). First openly bisexual statewide elected official.

- **John Berry** (1959–). Gay. US Ambassador to Australia (2013–).

- **James Costos** (1963–). Gay. US Ambassador to Spain (2013–).

- **Rufus Gifford**. Gay. US Ambassador to Denmark (2013–).

- **James "Wally" Brewster** (1960–). Gay. US Ambassador to the Dominican Republic (2013–).

- **Daniel Baer**. Gay. US Ambassador to the Organization for Security and Cooperation in Europe (2013–).

- **James Hormel** (1933–). Gay. Philanthropist. First openly LGBT ambassador to the United States (Luxembourg, 1999). Appointed during recess (Senate wouldn't confirm him).

- **Michael Guest** (1957–). Gay. Former US Ambassador to Romania (2001–2004). First openly gay ambassador to be confirmed by Senate. Retired in 2007 in protest for LGBT discrimination in the State Department.

- **Harvey Milk** (1930–1978). Gay. Member of San Francisco Board of Supervisors, who was murdered along with Mayor Moscone by a fellow supervisor.

- **Nancy Wechsler** (1950–). Lesbian. First open LGBT person elected to office in the United States (Ann Arbor City Council, 1972).

- **Angie Buhl** (1985–). Bisexual. Member, South Dakota State senate (2011–).

- **Micah Kellner** (1978–). Bisexual. Member, New York State Assembly (2007–).

- **JoCasta Zamarripa** (1976–). Bisexual. Member, Wisconsin State Assembly (2011–).

- **Waheed Alli** (1964–). Gay. Muslim. Member of the House of Lords, British Parliament.

- **J. Edgar Hoover** (1895–1972). Presumed gay. First director of the FBI (1935–1972).

- **Eleanor Roosevelt** (1882–1962). Presumed lesbian. First Lady of the United States (1933–1945).

- **Barbara Jordan** (1936–1996). Lesbian. Member of the US House of Representatives (1973–1979). Leader of the Civil Rights movement.

- **Deborah Batts** (1947–). Lesbian. First openly LGBT person to be appointed as federal judge (1994 by President Clinton).

- **Todd Hughes** (1960–). Gay. Fist openly LGBT person to be appointed to US Circuit Court.

- **Georgina Beyer** (1957–). Transgender. World's first open transgender individual to be elected to Parliament (New Zealand, 1999).

- **Edward II** (1284–1327). Bisexual. King of England.

- **Frederick the Great** (1712–1786). Presumed gay. King of Prussia (1772–1786).

- **Ferdinand I of Bulgaria** (1861–1948). Bisexual. Tsar of Bulgaria. Declared Bulgaria's independence from the Ottoman Empire.

RELIGION

- **Rev. Troy Perry** (1940–). Gay. Founder, Metropolitan Community Church.

- **Archbishop Carl Bean** (1944–). Gay. Founder, Unity Fellowship Church Movement. Made famous the song "I

Was Born This Way" in 1977, well before Lady Gaga.

- **Bishop Gene Robinson** (1947–). Gay. Episcopalian Bishop of New Hampshire—first of any major Christian religion.

- **Bishop Mary Douglas Glasspool** (1954–). Lesbian. First open lesbian to become bishop in the Anglican faith.

- **Bishop Guy Erwin**. Gay. Bishop, Evangelical Lutheran Church in America.

- **Rabbi Sharon Kleinbaum** (1959–). Lesbian. Senior Rabbi of the largest LGBT synagogue in the world.

- **Rabbi Stephen Greenberg** (1956–). Gay. First openly gay Orthodox rabbi.

- **Imam Daayiee Adfullah** (1954–). Gay. American Muslim imam. Co-director, Muslims for Progressive Values. Board member, Al-Fatiha Foundation.

- **Irshad Manji** (1968–). Lesbian. Canadian Muslim author, journalist, and advocate. Director of Moral Courage Project and NY University. Books: *Allah, Liberty and Love; The Trouble with Islam Today.* Documentary: *Faith Without Fear*

- **John McNeill** (1925–). Gay. Theologian and former Jesuit. Author of multiple books, notably *The Church and the Homosexual* (1976).

- **Rev. Malcolm Boyd** (1923–). Gay. Priest, author of more than thirty books, and civil rights activist. Came out in 1977.

- **Mel White** (1940–). Gay. Clergyman and writer: *Stranger at the Gate; Lust: The Other Side of Love.*

MILITARY

- **Alexander the Great** (356–323 BC). Presumed gay. Emperor, who by age thirty had expanded his domain from Greece to Persia and to Egypt. One of the most successful military commanders of all time.

- **Hadrian** (76–138 AD). Presumed gay. Fourteenth Emperor of the Roman Empire.

- **T. E. Lawrence, "Lawrence of Arabia"** (1888–1935). Presumed gay. Liaison during the Arab Revolt. Writer: *Seven Pillars of Wisdom.*

- **Tammy S. Smith** (1963–). Lesbian. Brigadier General, US Army. First openly LGBT general in the United States military.

SCIENCE

- **Alan Turing** (1912–1954). Gay. Father of computer science and artificial intelligence. Mathematical genius who broke German codes during WWII. His breakthroughs shortened WWII and saved thousands of lives.

- **Baron John Maynard Keynes** (1883–1946). Bisexual. One of the most influential economists ever.

- **Lynn Conway** (1938–). Transgender. Creator of the methodology used to design all computer chips. Also invented method for high-performance computers.

- **Sally Ride** (1951–2012). Lesbian. Astronaut, physicist, engineer, and educator. First American woman in space. Youngest American to go into space (age 32).

- **Joan Roughgarden** (1946–). Transgender. Professor emeritus of biology, Stanford University. Author of eight scientific books.

- **Ben Barres**. Transgender. Chair, Neurobiology, Stanford University School of Medicine.

- **Deirdre McCloskey** (1942–). Transgender. Professor of economics, University of Illinois at Chicago. Author of numerous books.

- **Nate Silver** (1978–). Gay. Statistician, blogger, author. Accurately predicted the 2008 and 2012 US elections.

SPORTS

- **Martina Navratilova** (1956–). Lesbian. Tennis player. All-time career record for men or women in singles and doubles.

- **Greg Louganis** (1960–). Gay. Four Olympic gold medals and five gold World Championships for diving. Best-selling author: *Breaking the Silence.*

- **Mildred "Babe" Zaharias** (1911–1956). Lesbian. One of the greatest athletes of the twentieth century. Two gold and one silver medals in 1932 Olympics. Multitalented: golf, basketball, track and field.

- **Sarah Vaillancourt** (1985–). Lesbian. Ice hockey player. Two Olympic gold metals.

- **Brian Boitano** (1963–). Gay. Olympic gold metal in figure skating.

- **Toller Cranston** (1949–). Gay. Figure skater. Canadian national champion. Bronze in 1976 Olympics.

- **Johnny Weir-Voronov** (1984–). Gay. American figure skater. Three time US national champion.

- **Renee Richards** (1934–). Transgender. Ophthalmologist, tennis player, and author.

- **Billie Jean King** (1943–). Lesbian. Professional tennis player.

- **Billy Bean** (1964–). Gay. Former Major League baseball player and author. Came out in 1999. Book: *Going the Other Way.*

- **Glenn Burke** (1952–1995). Gay. Former Major League baseball player. First and only Major League player known to be out to his team while a player.

- **Matthew Mitchman** (1988–). Gay. Olympic Gold for diving (2008) with the highest single-dive score in the history of the Olympics.

- **Tom Daley** (1994–). No Label. Olympic Bronze for diving (2012).

- **Ilana Kloss** (1956–). Lesbian. Tennis player. World Team Tennis commissioner.

- **Ian Roberts** (1965–). Gay. First rugby player to come out (1995).

- **Rosie Jones** (1959–). Lesbian. Golf player.

- **Orlando Cruz** (1981–). Gay. Professional boxer.

- **John Amaechi** (1974–). Gay. Basketball player.

- **Jason Collins** (1978–). Gay. Basketball player.

- **Robbie Rogers** (1987–). Gay. Soccer player.

- **Andrew Goldstein** (1983–). Gay. Lacrosse player.

BUSINESS

- **Sir Cecil Rhodes** (1853–1902). Presumed gay. Mining magnate. Founder of African state of Rhodesia. Funder of Rhodes scholarships.

- **Tim Cook** (1960–). Gay. CEO of Apple (2011–). One of the highest-paid executives ever ($376 million stock award in 2011).

- **Chris Hughes** (1983–). Gay. Cofounder, Facebook. Owner and publisher, *The New Republic*.

- **Peter Thiel** (1967–). Gay. Entrepreneur, venture capitalist, and hedge fund manager. Early investor in Facebook.

- **Tim Gill** (1953–). Gay. Cofounder of software company Quark. Philanthropist and activist: Gill Foundation and Gill Action, which together invest about $20 million a year to promote equality for LGBT people.

- **David Bohnett** (1956–). Gay. Cofounder of GeoCities, sold to Yahoo in 1999. His foundation has given more than $45 million in grants.

- **Jon Stryker** (1958–). Gay. Billionaire heir to Stryker corporation. Philanthropist.

- **Jonathan Lewis** (1958–). Gay. Progressive Insurance. Investor and visionary philanthropist.

- **Linda Ketner** (1950–). Lesbian. Heir to Food Lion's business. Management consultant and philanthropist.

- **Bruce Bastian** (1948–). Gay. Cofounder, WordPerfect. Philanthropist.

- **Martine Rothblatt** (1954–). Transgender. Attorney, author, and entrepreneur. Founder and CEO, United Therapeutics.

- **Kathy Levinson** (1956–). Lesbian. Former chief operating officer and president, E*Trade. Three-sport varsity athlete. Philanthropist.

- **Megan Smith** (1964–). Lesbian. Vice president, Google.

- **Mitchell Gold**. Gay. Cofounder, Mitchell Gold+Bob Williams furniture. Cofounder, Faith In America. Philanthropist. Author.

- **Bob Page** (1945–). Gay. Founder, Replacements Limited. Philanthropist.

- **Charles Merrill, Jr.** (1920–). Bisexual. Author, artist, and philanthropist. Son of Merrill-Lynch founder.

- **Michael Bishop** (1942–). Gay. Businessperson. Majority owner of BMI airline, which he sold to Lufthansa. Net worth around $800 million.

- **Kevin McClatchy** (1963–). Gay. Businessperson. Principal owner, Pittsburgh Pirates (1996–2007).

LITERATURE AND THEATER

- **William Shakespeare** (1564–1616). Presumed bisexual. Poet and playwright. Considered greatest writer in the English language.

- **Tennessee Williams** (1911–1983). Gay. Writer and playwright: *A Streetcar Named Desire, Cat on a Hot Tin Roof*, and more.

- **André Gide** (1869–1951). Gay. Writer. Literature Nobel Prize, 1947.

- **Hans Christian Anderson** (1805–1875). Presumed gay. Most famous writer of fairy tales.

- **Walt Whitman** (1819–1892). Gay. Father of free verse. One of the greatest American poets.

- **Virginia Woolf** (1882–1941). Lesbian. Writer: *Mrs. Dalloway, To the Lighthouse, Orlando, A Room of One's Own*, and more.

- **Truman Capote** (1924–1984). Gay. Writer: *Breakfast at Tiffany's, In Cold Blood,* and more.

- **Gore Vidal** (1925–2012). Gay. Writer: *The City and the Pillar, The Best Man, The Last Empire*, and more.

- **Ralph Waldo Emerson** (1803–1882). Bisexual. Writer. Leader of the Transcendentalist movement based on self-reliance.

- **E. M. Foster** (1879–1970). Gay. Novelist: *Where Angels Fear to Tread, The Longest Journey, A Room with a View, A Passage to India, Maurice,* and more.

- **Oscar Wilde** (1854–1900). Gay. Playwright and novelist: *The Importance of Being Earnest; Salome, The Picture of Dorian Gray,*

- **Thomas Mann** (1875–1955). Bisexual. Nobel Prize for Literature, 1929. Works: *Buddenbrooks, The Magic Mountain, Death in Venice,* and more.

- **James Baldwin** (1924–1987). Gay. Writer and civil rights activist. Books: *The Fire Next Time, Go Tell it on the Mountain,* and more.

- **Simone de Beauvoir** (1908–1986). Bisexual. Influential philosopher and writer. Companion of philosopher and author Jean-Paul Sartre.

- **Gertrude Stein** (1874–1946) and **Alice B. Toklas** (1877–1967). Lesbian couple. Writers, art collectors.

- **Dustin Lance Black** (1974–). Gay. Screenwriter. Oscar winner for *Milk* (Best Original Screenplay, 2008).

- **Sir Terence Rattigan** (1911–1977). Gay. Famous British playwright.

- **Harvey Fierstein** (1952–). Gay. Actor and playwright: *Torch Song Trilogy, La Cage aux Folles, A Catered Affair.*

- **Jean Cocteau** (1889–1963). Gay. French writer, artist, and filmmaker. Member: American Academy, French Academy, Royal Academy of Belgium, and German Academy.

- **Federico García Lorca** (1898–1936). Gay. Poet, dramatist, and theater director. One of the most important poets in the Spanish language.

- **Paul Verlaine** (1844–1896). Gay. Renowned French poet.

- **Arthur Rimbaud** (1854–1891). Gay. Prodigy French poet. Had long-term relationship with Paul Verlaine.

- **Armistead Maupin** (1944–). Gay. Writer: *Tales of the City* and more.

- **Alan Ball** (1955–). Gay. Writer, director, actor, producer. *American Beauty* (Oscar for Best Original Screenplay), *Six Feet Under.*

- **Andrew Tobias** (1947–). Gay. Writer about investments, coming out, other topics. Innovator in insurance. Treasurer, Democratic National Committee.

- **Reinaldo Arenas** (1943–1990). Gay. Best-selling writer of *Before Night Falls, Farewell to the Sea.*

- **W. H. Auden** (1907–1973). Gay. Famous poet.

MUSIC

- **Pyotr Ilyich Tchaikovsky** (1840–1893). Gay. Russian composer of classical music.

- **Leonard Bernstein** (1918–1990). Gay. Renowned American composer and conductor.

- **Sir Elton John** (1947–). Gay. Singer, songwriter, and composer.

- **"Lady Gaga"—Stefani Joanne Angelina Germanotta** (1986–). Bisexual. Singer, songwriter, producer, actress.

- **"Boy George"—George Alan O'Dowd** (1961–). Gay. Singer and songwriter.

- **George Michael** (1963–). Gay. Musician, singer and songwriter.

- **Cole Porter** (1891–1964). Gay. Composer and songwriter. Married Linda Lee Thomas. His parties in Paris were renowned.

- **Joan Baez** (1941–). Bisexual. Folksinger and songwriter.

- **Ricky Martin** (1971–). Gay. Singer and actor.

- **Whitney Houston** (1963–2012). Presumed bisexual. Singer. Actress. The most-awarded female act of all time.

PAINTING, SCULPTURE

- **Leonardo da Vinci** (1452–1519). Presumed gay. Painter, sculptor, architect, scientist, musician, and inventor. One of the greatest geniuses of all time.

- **Michelangelo** (1475–1564). Presumed gay. One of the most famous painters, sculptors, architects, poets, and engineers of the Renaissance.

- **Andy Warhol** (1928–1987). Gay. Artist. Leader of the Pop Art movement.

- **David Hockney** (1937–). Gay. Pop art painter, printmaker, and photographer.

FASHION

- **Cristobal Balenciaga** (1895–1972). Gay. Fashion designer. Founder of the Balenciaga *haute couture* house.

- **Gianni Versace** (1946–1997). Gay. Fashion designer. Founder of the Versace label.

- **Tom Ford** (1961–). Gay. Fashion designer. Founder of the Ford label. Movie Director: *A Single Man.*

- **Charles Nolan** (1957–2011). Gay. Fashion designer. Founder of the Nolan label.

MOVIES, ENTERTAINMENT, TV

- **Rock Hudson** (1925–1985). Gay. Actor who died of AIDS. His movies include: *Magnificent Obsession, Giant, Ice Station Zebra,* and *Dynasty.*

- **Sir Ian McKellen** (1939–). Gay. Actor.

- **George Takei** (1937–). Gay. Actor: *Star Trek.*

- **Angelina Jolie** (1975–). Bisexual. Actress, director, and humanitarian.

- **Ellen Degeneres** (1958–). Lesbian. Comedian, actress, TV show host.

- **Anderson Cooper** (1967–). Gay. Reporter, author, and TV anchor.

- **Rachel Maddow** (1973–). Lesbian. Author and TV host.

- **Don Lemon** (1966–). Gay. TV host.

- **Rosie O'Donnell** (1962–). Lesbian. TV show host, actress, comedian.

- **Cynthia Nixon** (1966–). Bisexual. Actress.

- **Alvin Ailey, Jr.** (1931–1989). Gay. Founder, Alvin Ailey American Dance Theater in New York.

- **Josephine Baker** (1906–1975). Bisexual. Singer, dancer, actress, and activist. Significant contributions to the Civil Rights movement.

- **Rudolph Valentino** (1895–1926). Presumed gay. Famous actor in silent movies. Known as the Latin Lover. Married twice to women who presumably had lesbian relationships.

- **Marlon Brando** (1924–2004). Presumed bisexual. Actor. Named by the American Film Institute as the fourth greatest male American actor of all times. The book *Brando Unzipped* claims he had relationships with other famous actors, including James Dean, Cary Grant, John Gielgud, and Montgomery Clift.

- **Cary Grant** (1904–1986). Bisexual. Actor. The American Film Institute named him the Greatest Male Star of All Time. Movies: *The Philadelphia Story; To Catch a Thief; An Affair to Remember; North by Northwest...*

- **Sir John Gielgud** (1904–2000). Gay. Actor, director, producer. One of few to win an Oscar, a Tony, an Emmy, and a Grammy.

- **Montgomery Clift** (1920–1966). Bisexual. Actor: *From Here to Eternity, A Place in the Sun, Confess,* and more. Nominated four times for Academy Awards.

- **Greta Garbo** (1905–1990). Bisexual. Actress: *Anna Christie, Grand Hotel.*

- **James Dean** (1931–1955). Gay. Iconic actor: *Rebel Without a Cause, East of Eden,* and *Giant.*

- **Anthony Perkins** (1932–1992). Gay. Oscar-winning actor. Died of AIDS.

- **Jodie Foster** (1962–). Lesbian. Actress, film director, and producer.

- **Sir Laurence Olivier** (1907–1989). Presumed bisexual. Renowned actor and director.

- **Tab Hunter** (1931–). Gay. Actor: *Battle Cry, That Kind of Woman.*

- **Laverne Cox**. Transgender. Actress, producer: *Orange is the New Black, Musical Chairs* and more.

- **Suze Orman** (1951–). Lesbian. Financial advisor, author, TV host.

- **David Geffen** (1943–). Gay. Film, theater, and music producer: *ET, Saving Private Ryan,* and more.

- **Chaz Bono** (1969–). Transgender. Writer and musician. Child of entertainers Sonny and Cher.

- **Ismail Merchant** (1936–2005) and **James Ivory** (1928–). Gay couple. Founders, Merchant Ivory productions. Films: *A Room with a View, Maurice, Mr. and Mrs. Bridge, Howards End.*

- **Pier Paolo Pasolini** (1922–1975). Gay. Film director and writer. Films: *Teorema, Canterbury Tales.*

- **Luchino Visconti** (1906–1976). Gay. Film, opera, and theater director. Films include *Death in Venice, The Leopard,* and *The Dammed.*

- **Pedro Almodóvar** (1949–). Gay. Oscar-winning Spanish filmmaker: *All About My Mother. Talk to Her.*

- **Lana Wachowski** (1965–). Transgender. Working as a team with brother Andy, they are filmmakers, screenwriters, and producers: The *Matrix* series of movies, and others.

- **James Randi** (1928–). Gay. Magician. Investigator of occult, paranormal, and supernatural claims.

CIVIC ENGAGEMENT

- **Harry Hay** (1912–2002). Gay. Renowned LGBT rights activist. Cofounder: Mattachine Society, Radical Faeries.

- **Del Martin** (1921–2008) and **Phyllis Lyon** (1924–). Lesbian couple. Renowned feminists and gay-rights activists. Founders of Daughters of Bilitis.

- **Frank Kameny** (1925–2011). Gay. Astronomer. Activist. Created slogan *"Gay is Good."*

- **Bayard Rustin** (1912–1987). Gay. Civil rights leader. Main organizer of the 1983 March on Washington.

- **Jane Addams** (1860–1935). Lesbian. First American woman to win the Nobel Peace Prize (1931).

- **Leonard Matlovich** (1943–1988). Gay. Vietnam War veteran, Purple Heart and Bronze Star. Tombstone reads: "A Gay Vietnam Veteran—When I was in the military, they gave me a medal for killing two men and a discharge for loving one."

- **Roberta Achtenberg** (1950–). Lesbian. First openly LGBT person whose appointment required US Senate confirmation (1993, asst. secretary of Housing and Urban Development). Currently, commissioner, US Commission on

Civil Rights.

- **Chai Feldblum** (1959–). Lesbian. Professor of law, Georgetown University. Chair, Equal Employment Opportunity Commission.

- **Axel and Eigil Axgil** (Axel: 1915–2011; Eigil: 1922–1995). Gay. First gay couple in the world to be joined in a registered domestic partnership (Denmark, 1989).

- **Ann Bancroft** (1955–). Lesbian. Adventurer, teacher, author. First woman to reach the North Pole by foot and sled. First woman to cross both the North and South Poles. First woman to ski across Greenland.

- **Baron Baden Powell** (1857–1941). Presumed gay. Army officer and writer. Considered the founder of the International Scouting Movement (Boy Scouts).

- **Laurence Michael Dillon** (1915–1962). Transgender. Physician, aristocrat, and first female-to-male transgender individual to undergo phalloplasty. Author: *Self—A Study in Endocrinology and Ethics.*

In addition, there are many other people who are committed to achieving equality for lesbian, gay, bisexual and transgender people. Here are just a few of them:

FOUNDERS OF NEW ORGANIZATIONS FOR EQUALITY (last 10 years)

- **Juan and Ken Ahonen-Jover** (eQualityGiving)

- **Tico Almeida** (Freedom to Work)

- **Wayne Besen** (Truth Wins Out)

- **Dana Beyer and Sharon Brackett** (Gender Rights Maryland)

- **David Brock** (EqualityMatters)

- **Linda Bush** (Movement Advancement Project)

- **Mitchell Gold and Jimmy Creech** (Faith in America)

- **Georg Ketelhohn and Heddy Pena + 12 more** (Florida Together)

- **Carolyn Laub** (Gay Straight Alliance Network)

- **Robyn McGeehe and Kip Williams** (GetEqual)

- **Dan Savage** (It Gets Better)

- **Josh Seefried and Ty Walrod** (OutServe, which merged with SLDN)

- **Chuck Williams** (The Williams Institute)

- **Shane Windmeyer, Chad Wilson,** and **Sarah Holmes** (Campus Pride)

HEADS OF MAJOR NATIONAL ORGANIZATIONS FOR EQUALITY

- **Michael Adams** (Services and Advocacy for LGBT Elders, SAGE)

- **Gregory T. Angelo** (Log Cabin Republicans, LCR)

- **Aaron Belkin** (Palm Center)

- **Gabriel Blau** (Family Equality Council)

- **Eliza Byard** (Gay Lesbian & Straight Education Network, GLSEN)

- **Rea Carey** (The Task Force)

- **Kevin Cathcart** (Lambda Legal)

- **Heather Cronk** and **Felipe Sousa-Rodriguez** (GetEqual)

- **Jerame Davis** (National Stonewall Democrats, NSD)

- **Masen Davis** (Transgender Law Center)

- **James Esseks** (American Civil Liberties Union LGBT Project)

- **Chad Griffin** (Human Rights Campaign, HRC)

- **Jody Huckaby** (Parents, Families and Friends of Lesbians and Gays, PFLAG)

- **Rebecca Isaacs** (Equality Federation)

- **Mara Keisling** (National Center for Transgender Equality, NCTE)

- **Kate Kendell** (National Center for Lesbian Rights, NCLR)

- **Sharon Lettman-Hicks** (National Black Justice Coalition, NBJC)

- **Abbe Land** (The Trevor Project)

- **Ricci Levy** (Woodhull Sexual Freedom Alliance)

- **Dave Montez** (GLAAD)

- **Darren Phelps** (Pride at Work)

- **Terry Stone** (CenterLink)

- **Lee Swislow**—retiring (Gay & Lesbian Advocates & Defenders, GLAD)

- **Rachel Tiven** (Immigration Equality)

- **Adam Umboefer** (American Foundation for Equal Rights, AFER)

- **Chuck Wolfe** (Victory Fund)

- **Evan Wolfson** (Freedom to Marry)

ACTIVISTS AND DONORS WHO ARE MAKING A DIFFERENCE

- **Henry van Ameringen,** strategic donor
- **Ron Ansin,** strategic donor
- **Chip Arndt,** activist and *Amazing Race* winner
- **John Bare,** activist donor
- **Jarrett Barrios,** strategist
- **Vic Basile,** strategist
- **Ignatius Bau,** strategist
- **Dana Beyer,** transgender activist and political candidate
- **Adam Bink,** grassroots activist
- **Mary Bonauto,** legal super ace
- **Marsha Botzer,** transgender activist
- **Jeff Campagna,** activist
- **Tom Carpenter,** strategist
- **Mandy Carter,** activist and Nobel Prize nominee
- **Jerry Chasen,** activist donor
- **Dan Choi,** DADT and equality activist
- **Bobby Clark,** online activist
- **Kate Clinton,** comedian
- **Michael Coe,** communicator
- **Matt Coles,** legal strategist
- **David da Silva Cornell,** activist
- **Anna Curren,** repeal DADT donor
- **Erin Drinkwater,** activist and doer
- **Stephen Driscoll,** democratic activist
- **Liebe and Seth Gadinsky,** allied donors
- **Brian Gaither,** activist
- **Chris Gates**, activist
- **Ethan Geto,** communications strategist
- **Don George,** activist donor
- **Lila Gracey,** strategist
- **Joe Falk,** political donor
- **J. Todd "Tif" Fernandez,** grassroots activist
- **Matt Foreman,** strategist
- **Nathaniel Frank,** author
- **Stephen Handwerk,** Democratic activist
- **Craig Harwood,** donor and producer
- **Yashar Hedayat,** strategic donor
- **Stephen Herbits,** strategic doer, and donor
- **Joanne Herman,** transgender educator
- **Daniel Hernandez,** helping hand
- **Kelly Rivera Hart,** Latino and bi activist

- **Steve Hildebrand,** strategist
- **Donald Hitchcock,** strategist and activist
- **Ernest Hopkins,** activist
- **Bob Horvath,** political activist
- **Lane Hudson,** communications strategist and provocateur
- **Kathy James,** family advocate
- **Brian Johnson,** activist
- **Corey Johnson,** activist and political candidate
- **Hans Johnson,** activist
- **Michael Kenny,** strategist and connector
- **Norm Kent,** publisher
- **Jon Kislak,** allied donor
- **Geoff Kors,** strategist
- **Lisa Kove,** Department of Defense activist
- **Michael Krawitz,** strategic donor
- **Janice Langbehn,** activist and 2011 US presidential Citizens medal recipient
- **Andrew Lane,** foundation executive director
- **Jeff Lewy,** activist donor
- **Kerry Lobel,** strategist
- **Bill Lyons,** donor advisor
- **Barbara McCullough-Jones,** activist
- **Stuart Milk,** international activist
- **Richard Milstein,** donor
- **Shannon Price Minter,** transgender legal ace
- **Ineke Mushovic,** strategist
- **Kathryn Natale and Janet McLeod,** strategic donors
- **Christopher Neff,** journalist and publisher
- **Richard Noble,** walking activist
- **Derek Newton,** allied campaign strategist
- **CJ Ortuno,** activist ally
- **Dixon Osburn,** strategist
- **Kathy Padilla,** transgender activist
- **Jim Pepper,** strategic donor
- **Catherine Pino** and **Ingrid Duran,** strategists
- **Libby Post,** communicator
- **Bruce Presley,** donor and producer
- **Lisa Polyak,** marriage activist
- **Gautam Raghavan,** White House liaison
- **Donna Red Wing,** activist leader
- **Cathy Renna,** communications expert
- **Alix Ritchie and Marty Davis,** agitators
- **Laura Ricketts,** strategic donor
- **Cindy Rizzo,** human sexuality activist

- **Charles Robbins,** youth advocate
- **Mike Rogers,** blogger and citizen reporter
- **Charlie Rounds** and **Mark Hiemenz,** maverick donors
- **Hilary Rosen,** strategist
- **Marty Rouse,** grassroots activist
- **Caitlin Ryan,** family advocate and researcher
- **Rebecca Salokar,** professor and strategist
- **Diego Sanchez,** transgender activist
- **Marsha Scott,** donor strategist
- **Eugene Sepulveda,** donor
- **Garry Shay,** Democratic activist
- **Ken Sherrill,** political scientist
- **Joel Silberman,** media strategist
- **Howard Simon,** allied defender
- **Maryann Simpson,** donor
- **Barbra "Babs" Casbar Siperstein,** political compromiser
- **Richard Socarides,** activist
- **Palm Spaulding,** blogger
- **Rick Stafford,** Democratic activist
- **Anne Stanback,** marriage activist
- **Mark Steinberg** and **Dennis Edwards,** donors
- **Jim Stork,** strategist and donor
- **Sean Strub,** HIV activist
- **Andrew Sullivan,** author
- **Andy Szekeres,** fundraiser
- **Maxim Thorne,** strategist
- **Lisa Turner,** strategist
- **Urvashi Vaid,** author and strategist
- **Leoni Walker,** donor
- **Jillian Weiss,** transgender activist
- **Bernard Whitman,** communications expert
- **Sara Whitman,** activist donor
- **Jon Winkleman,** political activist
- **Bob Witeck,** communications expert
- **Paul Yandura,** donor strategist and revolutionary
- **Rich Yurko,** activist

APPENDIX 2:

The Dallas Principles

Below is the full text of the Dallas Principles (available at www.TheDallasPrinciples.com).

It is composed of: preamble, principles, full civil rights goals, and a call to action. The list of authors follows.

PREAMBLE

President Obama and Congress pledged to lead America in a new direction that included civil rights for lesbian, gay, bisexual and transgender Americans. We now sit at a great moment in our history that inspires the nation to return to its highest ideals and greatest promise. We face a historic opportunity to obtain our full civil rights; this is the moment for change. No delay. No excuses.

Nearly forty years ago, a diverse group of lesbian, gay, bisexual, and transgender people stood up to injustice at the Stonewall Inn in New York City. In doing so, they submitted themselves to bodily harm and criminal prosecution. Their demand was simple—equal protection under the law.

Still today, full civil rights has eluded the same community that rioted forty years ago. Instead, untold sums of resources have been spent to divide our nation and turn our lives into a political football.

At several junctures in American history, the stars have aligned to deliver the promise of equal protection under the law to those previously denied. At this unique time in history, our nation must once again exercise the great tradition of making its people equal.

Justice has too long been delayed. A clear path toward full civil equality for the LGBT community is overdue and must come now.

Using fear and misunderstanding to justify discrimination is no longer acceptable in this nation. Those content with the way things are will be judged harshly by history. Those who do not actively advance these ideals or offer excuses will be judged just as harshly. Those who attempt to divide our community or to delay and deny action on civil equality, waiting for the right moment to arrive, will be held accountable.

We reject the idea that honoring the founding principles of our country is controversial. We believe in the inherent human dignity of all people. No longer will we submit our children, our family, our friends, and ourselves as a political tool for any Party or ideology. A new day has arrived.

PRINCIPLES

The following eight guiding principles underlie our call to action. In order to achieve full civil rights now, we avow:

1. Full civil rights for lesbian, gay, bisexual and transgender individuals must be enacted now. Delay and excuses are no longer acceptable.

2. We will not leave any part of our community behind.

3. Separate is never equal.

4. Religious beliefs are not a basis upon which to affirm or deny civil rights.

5. The establishment and guardianship of full civil rights is a non-partisan issue.

6. Individual involvement and grassroots action are paramount to success and must be encouraged.

7. Success is measured by the civil rights we all achieve, not by words, access or money raised.

8. Those who seek our support are expected to commit to these principles.

FULL CIVIL RIGHTS GOALS

Being united by common principles and engaging in united action, we will achieve the following goals:

1. DIGNITY AND EQUALITY. Every lesbian, gay, bisexual, and transgender person has inherent dignity and worth, and has the right to live free of discrimination and harassment.

2. FAMILY. Every LGBT person has the right to a family without legal barriers to immigration, civil marriage, or raising children.

3. ECONOMIC OPPORTUNITY. Every LGBT person has the right to economic opportunity free from discrimination in employment, public housing, accommodation, public facilities, credit, and federally funded programs and activities.

4. EDUCATION. Every LGBT child and youth has the right to an education that is affirming, inclusive, and free from bullying.

5. NATIONAL SECURITY. Every LGBT person should have the opportunity to serve our

country openly and equally in our military and foreign service.

6. CRIME. Every LGBT person should enjoy life protected against bias crimes.

7. HEALTHCARE. Every person should have access to affordable, high quality, and culturally competent healthcare without discrimination.

CALL TO ACTION

1. We demand that government officials act now to achieve full civil rights without delay.

2. Our organizations and individuals need to develop a collaborative and revolutionary new organizing model that mobilizes millions of supporters through emerging web and phone technologies.

3. All LGBT individuals must accept personal responsibility to do everything within their power for equality and should get involved in the movement by volunteering, giving and being out.

4. We will hold elected officials and our organizations accountable for being transparent and achieving full civil rights by active participation when possible and active opposition when necessary.

5. Our allies need to be proactive in public support for full civil rights.

6. Every government measure that quantifies the US citizenry must permit LGBT individuals to self-identify and be counted in every way citizens are counted.

7. We demand that the media present LGBT lives in fair, accurate, and objective ways that neither include nor give credence to unsubstantiated, discriminatory claims and opinions.

AUTHORS

Here are the authors of the Dallas Principles with their affiliations at the time the principles were written.

- **Juan Ahonen-Jover, Ph.D.,** cofounder of eQualityGiving

- **Ken Ahonen-Jover, M.D.,** cofounder of eQualityGiving

- **John Bare,** activist donor

- **Senator Jarrett Barrios,** former Massachusetts legislator

- **Dana Beyer, M.D.,** transgender and political activist

- **Jeff Campagna, Esq.,** attorney and LGBT fundraiser and organizer

- **Mandy Carter,** Nobel Peace Prize nominee and lesbian activist

- **Michael Coe,** one of the "Most Influential Washingtonians under the Age of 40" according to *Washington Life Magazine*

- **Rev. Jimmy Creech,** straight ally working to end religion-based bigotry

- **Allison Duncan,** donor advisor

- **Ambassador Michael Guest,** senior advisor to the Council for Global Equality

- **Joanne Herman,** donor and transgender rights advocate

- **Donald Hitchcock,** activist and former executive director, Gay and Lesbian Leadership Council

- **Lane Hudson,** political activist and one of the "Most Influential Gay People in America" according to *Out Magazine*

- **Charles Merrill,** philanthropist (Merrill-Lynch family), activist, and artist

- **Dixon Osburn, Esq.,** cofounder, former executive director, Servicemembers Legal Defense Network

- **Lisa Polyak,** lead plaintiff in litigation to obtain marriage equality in Maryland

- **Babs Casbar Siperstein,** transgender activist and board member

- **Pam Spaulding,** editor and publisher, www.PamsHouseBlend.com

- **Andy Szekeres,** political consultant and fundraiser

- **Lisa Turner,** political consultant and donor advisor

- **Jon Winkleman,** political activist

- **Paul Yandura,** political strategist and donor advisor

APPENDIX 3:

Good Companies

Listed below by industry are the companies with a 100-percent rating in the 2014 Corporate Equality Index compiled by the Human Rights Campaign (www.hrc.org/cei). Note that this list is not exhaustive since there might be companies with a 100-percent rating that have not reported to the Human Rights Campaign.

ADVERTISING AND MARKETING
- Digitas
- Interpublic Group of Companies
- Leo Burnett Company (new)
- MSLGROUP Americas (new)
- Publicis Healthcare Communications (new)
- Publicis
- Razorfish
- Starcom MediaVest Group
- ZenithOptimedia (new)

AEROSPACE AND DEFENSE
- Boeing (new)
- Lockheed Martin
- Raytheon

AIRLINES
- AMR Corp. (American Airlines)
- United Continental Holdings

APPAREL, FASHION, TEXTILES, DEPARTMENT STORES
- Levi Strauss & Co.
- Nike

AUTOMOTIVE
- Chrysler
- Ford
- General Motors

- Nissan North America (new)
- Toyota
- Wolkswagen Group of America

BANKING AND FINANCIAL SERVICES
- American Express
- Ameriprise Financial
- Bank of America
- Bank of New York Mellon
- Barclays
- BlacRock
- BMO Bankcorp
- BNP Paribas
- Capital One
- Charles Schwab
- Citigroup
- Credit Suisse USA
- Depository Trust & Clearing Corp.
- Deutsche Bank
- Discover Financial Services (new)
- Eastern Bank (new)
- Freddie Mac
- Goldman Sachs
- HSBC - North America
- Huntington Bancshares
- JP Morgan Chase
- KeyCorp
- MasterCard
- Moody's
- Morgan Stanley
- Northern Trust
- PNC Financial Services Group
- RBC Capital Markets (new)
- RBC Wealth Management
- SunTrust Banks
- TD Bank
- Teachers Insurance & Annuity Association
- Toyota Financial Services
- US Bancorp
- UBS AG
- Union Bank (new)
- Wells Fargo

CHEMICALS AND BIOTECHNOLOGY
- BASF (new)
- Dow Chemical
- E.I. du Pont (new)
- Ecolab
- Genentech
- Monsanto

COMPUTER AND DATA SERVICES
- Automatic Data Processing
- Broadridge Financial Solutions
- EMC
- Hewlett-Packard
- Tech Data

COMPUTER HARDWARE AND OFFICE EQUIPMENT
- Apple
- Dell
- Lexmark International
- Xerox

COMPUTER SOFTWARE
- CA Technologies
- Electronic Arts
- Intuit
- Microsoft
- Oracle
- Salesforce.com (new)
- SAP America (new)
- Symantec

CONSULTING AND BUSINESS SERVICES
- A.T. Kearney
- Accenture
- Aon
- Bain & Co./Bridgespan Group
- Booz Allen Hamilton
- Boston Consulting Group
- Deloitte
- Ernst & Young
- Huron Consulting Group (new)
- IBM
- KPMG
- Marsh & McLennan Companies

- McKinsey & Co.
- Navigant Consulting
- Nielsen (new)
- PricewaterhouseCoopers
- Thomson Reuters

EDUCATION AND CHILD CARE
- Bright Horizons Family Solutions (new)

ENERGY AND UTILITIES
- Exelon
- PG&E
- Portland General Electric (new)
- Sempra Energy
- Southern California Edison

ENGINEERING AND CONSTRUCTION
No companies in this industry reporting 100 percent rating

ENTERTAINMENT AND ELECTRONIC MEDIA
- AMC Entertainment
- SIRIUS XM Radio (new)
- Sony Pictures Entertainment
- Time Warner
- Viacom (new)
- Walt Disney

FOOD, BEVERAGES AND GROCERIES
- Brown-Forman
- Campbell Soup (new)
- Cargill
- Coca-Cola
- Darden Restaurants
- Delhaize America
- Diageo North America
- E&J Gallo Winery
- General Mills
- Kellogg
- Kraft Foods
- Land O'Lakes (new)
- MillerCoors
- PepsiCo
- Safeway (new)
- Sodexo

FOREST AND PAPER PRODUCTS
No companies in this industry reporting 100 percent rating

HEALTHCARE / HEALTH INSURANCE
- Aetna
- Blue Cross Blue Shield of Minnesota
- Cardinal Health
- CareFusion (new)
- Group Health Cooperative
- Group Health Permanente (new)
- Humana (new)
- Kaiser Permanente
- McKesson (new)
- UnitedHealth Group

HEALTHCARE / MEDICAL FACILITIES
No companies in this industry reporting 100 percent rating

HIGH-TECH / PHOTO / SCIENCE EQUIPMENT
- Cisco
- Eastman Kodak
- Medtronic
- Nokia

HOME FURNISHING
- Mitchell Gold + Bob Williams

HOTELS, RESORTS AND CASINOS
- Caesars Entertainment
- Choice Hotels International
- Hilton Worldwide (new)
- Hyatt Hotels
- Kimpton Hotel & Restaurant Group
- Marriott International (new)
- MGM Resorts
- Starwood Hotels & Resorts
- The Cosmopolitan of Las Vegas (new)
- Wyndham Worldwide
- Wynn Resorts

INSURANCE
- AAA Northern California, Nevada & Utah Insurance
- AIG
- AXA Equitable Life Insurance (new)

- Blue Cross and Blue Shield of Florida
- Chubb
- CIGNA
- Hartford Financial Services
- Harvard Pilgrim Health Care
- ING North America Insurance
- Massachusetts Mutual Life Insurance (new)
- MedLife
- Nationwide
- Progressive
- Prudential Financial
- Sun Life Financial (U.S.)

INTERNET SERVICES AND RETAILING
- eBay
- Groupon
- Google
- Yahoo!

LAW FIRMS
Eighty-one law firms report a 100 percent rating (ten more than in 2013 and twenty-six more than in 2012)

MAIL AND FREIGHT DELIVERY
No companies in this industry reporting 100 percent rating

MANUFACTURING
- Corning
- Cummins
- Danaher (new)
- General Electric (new)
- Herman Miller
- Owens Corning
- Rockwell Automation
- United Technologies
- Whirlpool

MINING AND METALS
- Alcoa

MISCELLANEOUS
- Sony Electronics (new)

OIL AND GAS
- Chevron

PHARMACEUTICALS
- Biogen Idec (new)
- Boehringer Ingelheim USA
- Bristol-Myers Squibb
- Eli Lilly
- GlaxoSmithKline
- Johnson & Johnson
- Merck
- Novartis Pharmaceuticals
- Pfizer

PUBLISHING AND PRINTING
- Pearson (new)

REAL ESTATE, COMMERCIAL
- CBRE (new)

REAL ESTATE, RESIDENTIAL
No companies in this industry reporting 100 percent rating

RETAIL AND CONSUMER PRODUCTS
- 3M
- A|X Armani Exchange (new)
- Abercrombie & Fitch
- American Eagle Outfitters (new)
- Avon
- Barnes & Noble
- Best Buy
- Clorox
- GameStop
- Gap
- Limited Brands
- Nordstrom
- Office Depot
- Procter & Gamble (new)
- Replacements
- Sears
- Staples
- Target (new)
- Uniliver
- Walgreens

TELECOMMUNICATIONS
- Alcatel-Lucent
- AT&T
- Comcast
- QUALCOMM
- Sprint
- Time Warner Cable
- T-Mobile USA
- Verizon

TOBACCO
No companies in this industry reporting 100 percent rating

TRANSPORTATION AND TRAVEL
- Orbitz

WASTE MANAGEMENT
No companies in this industry reporting 100 percent rating